The Sho Nuff Blues

J Yvonne

ISBN: 0692809988
ISBN 13: 9780692809983

I dedicate these words to
all the rainbows in the sky and
I put this on everything
I love.

I'm Gonna Take What He's Got

THE SUNLIGHT MADE its grand appearance through the large Cathedral windows. I tried hard to get in a few extra moments of sleep, but the more I tried the harder the sun rays pierced through my eyelids. I adjusted my body to the most comfortable position in the deep seated thick cushioned couch but still no luck. The brightness of the sun and my sore back worked together to send a message that it was time to wake up. I was so comfortable in my uncomfortable position, and I chose to ignore the signals a little while longer.

My body remained still and stiff as a board. We left the television on all night and I could hear a passionate debate. My mind made a deal between my eyes and ears. If I was interested in the conversation, I would listen with my eyes closed. If the conversation bored me it was time to wake up.

I listened and became pissed. Same sex marriage headlined the show. I rolled my eyes open and flexed my lips to the side and forced my eyes shut. A panel of same sex union supporters argued for their love and for the love of their friends and the opposition argued the morality of the issue.

The source of my unrest did not originate from either side of the panel. I decided that I was totally against same sex marriage. Not because of my moral concerns. I had enough real sins of my own to worry about the perception of someone else's. I was categorically against it because I would be damned if my hair stylist married a man before I did.

My boyfriend's couch always left knots in my back so I stretched out the kinks from side to side before standing. Ryan left before daybreak. The night before he mentioned something about a busted water pipe at one of his rental properties. He made a point to leave early so that we would not be late for church, and I had overslept.

I folded the blankets on the couch and stored them in Ryan's bedroom. His bedroom was three times the size of the sitting room that we slept in. And it would be one thing if we just so happened to fall asleep in the sitting room while watching a movie but the truth of the matter is that we always slept there on the nights that I stayed over. I hated Ryan's bedroom, and I refused to sleep in his bed. His bedroom was full of unpleasant surprises and no matter what the temperature registered, I always felt cold there.

Ryan accepted the couch as our bed together. Our son was too young to notice the irony of the arrangement and my daughter's 10-year-old lens was too innocent to focus on it. The kids and I lived with Ryan on the weekends and lived in our condo in the city during the weekdays. It was a hard routine choreographed by Ryan. We waltzed through most of it, tripped over a few steps, but we always moved through the motions. And the motion of today called for me to get myself and the kids ready for church.

I only went in his bedroom to get dressed. I walked through the room and resisted the urge to look at the folded pieces of paper that littered the dresser. I walked into his bathroom which was twice as large as the kitchen in my condo. I heard little feet shuffling towards me and Cody, our two year old son, joined me in the bathroom.

"Good Morning, mommy's little man"

My smile made him giggle, and he reached for me to pick him up. I grabbed him and his swollen diaper. Before he entered into his full play zone, I washed him up, changed his weighted diaper and put his church clothes on. While I was in route to wake up Cassidy, my cell phone rang and I answered Ryan's call.

"What's your status?"

"I am not dressed or Cassidy, but Cody has his clothes on. Are you finished fixing the pipe?"

"No, but I picked up one of my workers and the materials and I'm heading home, I can't believe this shit, I had to spend two hundred dollars this morning and the tenants haven't paid rent in six months."

"Why won't you have them evicted?"

"Well, when they get their section 8 voucher back that's guaranteed money."

"But they haven't had it in six months, why do you think they will ever get their section 8 situations taken care of?"

"That's a good point, I will give them another month and then they have to go." Ryan was always giving me credit for making good points, yet he only followed my advice as a last resort. Then he would say, "You told me to do that didn't you." And I wouldn't let my mouth say, "I told you so," but my eyes would.

"Anyway, will you be ready to go when I get home, you know it will only take me fifteen minutes and I will be ready to walk out the door."

"Yes, we will be ready." I said as I rolled my eyes.

I knocked on the door to the room formerly known as Cassidy's. We referred to it as "Cassidy's room" because this is where my daughter slept when we spent the weekend with Ryan. It lacked any signs of Cassidy other than a few outfits that hung in the closet. The bed ensemble was a black Lacquer mirror and dresser with a matching headboard. The full sized bed was covered by a cheap paisley comforter set that Ryan bought for himself during his senior year of college. I didn't attempt to redecorate this room or any room in the house for this matter. After all, I knew that I was only a visitor, no matter what he said about his intentions for our family, his inactions and actions were always consistent, and although I was holding on to the idea of our family, every day I felt my grip slipping.

"Good morning Sunshine, rise and shine."

"Can I just stay here?"

"So you can play the Sims on computer all morning, absolutely not."

"Ugh." She struggled to open her eyes. You would think she worked the night shift.

"Get up Cassidy, your clothes are on the ironing board."

My daughter was a typical 10-year-old, and her love for the Lord had not yet caught up to her love for sleeping in and playing computer games. She rolled out of bed and started to get dressed.

I went into the kitchen and seasoned a chuck roast, with onions, spices and green peppers. I rewashed the mixed green that I had picked from the night before and seasoned a pot of water with smoked turkey bottoms and spices just the way my grandmother taught me. The only real evidence of a women's presence in Ryan's house was the spices in the kitchen. I didn't leave one single female flag, like tampons, nail polish, or body wash in his bathroom. I knew I was on borrowed time. I just didn't have the energy to keep the weekend thing going. Whenever I decided that I didn't want to do this shit anymore, I didn't want to have to pack up a lot of stuff like the last time. Hell, he can keep the spices.

A man who has a beautiful home, a nice car and money in the bank on an average day, should be able to afford a family but not according to Ryan. The economy had "fucked us all up and he would feel perfectly comfortable with us getting married if banks were lending money to small business." Now was just not a good time for him to spend thousands of dollars at one time. He needed to have access to all of his liquid assets, but he assured me that I had nothing to worry about in terms of his level of commitment to me. Marriage, "was just a technicality," so in essence, I need not question him about marriage. Only have faith that one day it would come, like the return of Jesus.

Paying careful attention to the time, I put on my church clothes. It was nothing fancy, just a pair of black pants and a yellow button up collared shirt. Cassidy wore a dress with yellow and other pastels, and Cody wore a gray sweater. Ryan finished his business with his tenant, and just as he promised was dressed in 15 minutes. He wore a pair of khaki pants and a burnt orange sweater. Somehow we always managed to miss out on coordinating color schemes for our clothes.

We made it to church late but in time to hear the church's announcements, the altar call, three selections from the choir, the pastor's sermon and the benediction. Whatever came before all that, the Holy Spirit probably missed too. I felt that the message was clear and on point with what we needed to hear. The pastor preached about living for the future and he said, "Your windshield is so much larger than your rear view mirror because your blessings are all ahead and they are endless, while your rear view mirror is for you to take a quick glance back and only to avoid danger." Ryan made such a big deal about making it to church on time. I couldn't wait to hear his take on the pastor's sermon.

"So what did you think about the message?" I asked.

"Well it was okay. It was more inspirational than a message about God. I like the pastor, but the choir needs work."

Looking out the window, I'd answered my own question for Ryan's purpose for going to church. He was not there for deliverance. He came to church for entertainment, and if by chance the Lord would forgive him for a sin or two that would be an added bonus. I closed my eyes and pretended to sleep all the way to my weekend home.

It didn't take long before we were at Ryan's two-story, 4,000 square foot suburban home. He didn't live far from my father's home, and I was proud of Ryan for being able to purchase a home in the neighborhood my dad spent his entire working life to afford.

The trees showed signs of the early fall and the air was light and cool enough for a jacket but warm enough to stroll the neighborhood.

"Hey babe, let's go for a walk with the kids." On the outside we looked like a family that took long Sunday walks and my request matched our image.

"Sure, sweetheart, he said in his Leave-It-To-Beaver voice with a touch of sarcasm.

"Okay let me just change into some comfortable clothes and check on dinner." I knew that I was looking forward to the walk just a little bit more than Ryan, but I didn't mind. I always hoped that moments like these would add up to Ryan recognizing the beauty of us having a stable family. Cassidy opted out of the walk and went inside to play a game on the computer.

Cody drove recklessly ahead of us in his power wheel, and we talked. Well, he talked, and I listened. He complained about his employees, his tenants, the cost of labor, the cost of materials, the government, the price of gas, the banks, his mother, his father, his sister, his cousins, his aunties, and his uncles. I don't remember my exact responses, but I'm pretty sure that at the end of his laundry list of complaints, I told him that everything would be alright. The walk did not go as I'd planned it in mind. I was hoping for a line or two of us expressing how much we cared about each other. However, his complaints didn't leave any space for that.

Dinner was just about finished and Ryan invited his parent over. He told them dinner would be ready at 4:30. This meant that they would be there at 4:15, which was very normal in society, but not in my family. Our meeting times always had an ish at the end of them like 6ish or 7ish, and the actual time was not relevant because our events didn't end.

I sliced a few yams. The last yam almost killed me. I almost chopped my finger off. I threw away the blood stained yams and bandaged my index finger. The remaining yams were sprinkled with butter and sugar and spices and placed in the oven. Eventually, the

THE SHO NUFF BLUES

yams would candy and some of the edges would turn crispy and the center of the yam would be slightly chewy. I mixed a six generation buttermilk cornbread recipe and baked it in a cast iron skillet. What went into that skillet could slow Jiffy down. The cornbread reached a golden brown and the yams did exactly what I knew they would and it was just passed 4:00 pm.

As anticipated at 4:15, Ryan's mother was at the door. Trailing her in a separate car, Ryan's father followed.

"Where is my little stinker?" Nana said with a smile and Cody's legs moved as fast as they could to greet his Nana.

"Well, everything is ready. We can eat." I brushed my hands on my apron and looked back at my pots.

Ryan pulled out plates and glasses for everyone and made everyone's plate. He made sure he touched my shoulder or patted my ass whenever he was in arm's reach. While everyone's attention zoomed in on Cody, Ryan jokingly licked the side of my face. I lightly slapped him and wiped the spit off my cheek. With everyone's plate set in front of them, Nana prayed over the food. We ate ourselves into a food stupor but everyone continued to return to the pots for a little bit more of this or that. We sat at the table in the formal dining area of the house. The walls were painted a deep red color, and there was a walnut china cabinet with Ryan's old basketball trophies on several shelves and important papers on others. The dinner table conversation was semi-scripted and safe. I answered a standard set of questions from Ryan's mother.

"How's your grandmother?"

"How's your mother?"

"Is your stepmother still a nurse at the same hospital?"

"What's your brother been up to?"

"Is your nephew still in the hospital?"

"How is your job going?"

Nana was a genuinely sweet woman, and she always checked to make sure every family member that I ever introduced her to

was in good health. If there was a member of my family celebrating a milestone, she was right there with us, and whenever something was wrong, she was right there to help. Plus if it wasn't for
her small talk, Ryan and his father would have dominated the conversation with a complaining cypher. Between, Ryan or his dad I
couldn't tell who complained the most. The increase cost of gas,
local politics, state politics, federal politics and the color blue
were all hot topics and major points of contention for their lives.
If this wasn't like this then this wouldn't be like that was the huge
verbal ball that they tossed back and forth. The more they talked,
the more you could tell that Ryan did not respect his father's opin-
ions and his father didn't respect his. So to keep the peace I came
up with my own standard series of questions to ask Nana. The pale
conversations and carbs made everyone excuse themselves one
by one to other areas of the house. Cassidy went to the computer
room. Nana and Papa sat at opposite poles of the family room and
Ryan and I sat next to each other on the couch.

As a married couple, this scene would have been just a moment
of preparation to a busy week ahead, but as a couple that can be best
described as a boyfriend and girlfriend with a toddler aged son, this
scene marked the end of the weekend and the end of the era in which
I played weekend wife.

Nana was the proud mother of Ryan and if anyone in the world
would be aware of Ryan's intentions to marry me it would be her. So
I initiated a conversation to gauge a realistic timeline for a proposal.
This conversation along with the current issue of the Bloomberg
report should give me a more accurate approximation for a real wedding date.

"Nana," I called her attention and looked at her with childlike eyes.

"Yes," she answered with curiosity because I had never addressed
her like this.

"Did you know that Ryan and I are getting married soon?"

With surprise and pity in her eyes she replied, "No, no, no I did not."

"Well did you know that we were talking about marriage?"

"Not really, but I figured that you should."

"Well, we have been, and your son says the only reason why we are not engaged at this moment is because he wants to buy me a beautiful ring, and it's just not a good time to just drop 15 stacks on a ring."

She turned to her son, and he exchanged an off guard look with her and his father's eyes shifted between the three of us.

"What is 15 stacks?" Her cheeks lifted and her eyebrows sank as she tried to solve the 15 stack riddle.

"Fifteen thousand dollars." I answered

"Well son, the cost of the ring does not matter. You can always upgrade later."

"That is exactly what I told him Nana, but he told me that he wanted to buy me a beautiful ring and this is why we are not married or engaged."

There was awkward silence in the air, and I started an eye contact contest with Ryan that I was not going to lose.

"Don't worry your pretty little heart," Ryan chimed in. "I am not going anywhere."

Whatever that was supposed to mean to me, I didn't have the proper upbringing to respect or understand. In Ryan's mind, the last statement should satisfy the requirements of this conversation. The strangest thing ever was that his dad never uttered a word and for this reason I wanted to cut his father's head open, just to see if there was anything in it. There is no chance in hell that my father would have listened to any of my brothers say to their child's mother, "that they are not going anywhere," as a measure to defer a proposal. My father would literally stand up out of his chair and point directly in the face of my brother and say with bass and squinted eyes, "Well you should marry her." But Ryan's father just sat there and watched the show. I should have popped him some popcorn.

The attention turned to the television, and the thought of my upcoming one-hour journey to the city started to piss me off. At that moment, I wished that I was on TV. I wished that I was on Meet the Press petitioning for mandatory marriage and pensions for dedicated jump-offs.

Reality pie had been served for dessert, and I was slowly starting to digest it. I had four loads of laundry that were waiting for me at home and Cassidy told me that she had a homework assignment that she forgot to pack on Friday. I envied Ryan's ability to sink into the couch and channel surf. He was just way too comfortable. Ryan looked very well settled, and although I didn't have the Bloomberg report in my hand, the conversation that I had with Nana let me know that Ryan could live like this for years. Damn, he has it good, I thought and in that very moment I decided to serve this weekend marriage with invisible weekend divorce papers. I'm not doing this shit anymore I promised myself. I didn't promise to leave him completely, but I decided to stop playing the happy weekend wife.

I went into the master bedroom and made sure I hadn't left anything behind. I checked every drawer and removed my expectations and hope from each one. In his nightstand, right beside my expectations and hope were an opened box of condoms that were not used with me. Well, he promised not to go anywhere, but he didn't say he wouldn't invite anyone over. I didn't have the time nor mental space to address this, so I didn't even take the condoms out of the drawer. I held a poker face, masking the pain that my heart felt.

"Cassidy, come on it's time to go."

She appeared and dryly said goodbye to Ryan and his parents and then went to look for a missing shoe. I stuffed our bags in my car. Ryan carried Cody to the car and buckled him into his car seat. I sat in the driver seat impatiently waiting on Cassidy to find her left shoe. Finally, she appeared in the passenger front seat. Ryan gave me a kiss on the lips, and I backed out of the driveway. I looked out of my rear view mirror and made sure that I did not touch the meticulous lawn behind me. *Who fucking has that much time to invest in grass. And as I drove through super suburbia on steroids, I mentally plucked out everyone's grass, blade by blade... Fuck they grass.*

Times A Wastin

SUNDAY EVENINGS ALWAYS made a mockery of the weekends I spent with Ryan. Weekends were designed for enjoying time with your family and friends and more importantly, organizing your life to set the stage for a productive upcoming week. I had around two hours to accomplish all of the things that I should have finished over the past two days. Somewhere in time and space there was a coo coo clock personalized just for me. Every time the hour changed, a dodo bird popped out. Instead of chiming or singing the bird repeated, "You are always rushing." And at 7 o'clock, I heard the clock chant this line seven times. I could feel 9 o'clock breathing down my shoulders.

I didn't expect the cleaning fairy to come to my home while I was away the entire weekend, but it sure would have helped. Overall, my home was not cluttered, but four loads of laundry were waiting patiently for me. The hardwood floors couldn't hide another footprint or spill. And the bathrooms were clean enough for all deposits, but not suitable for putting on makeup or brushing your teeth. I set an impossible goal and told myself that I would be able to clean the entire house and put my children to bed all before 9 o'clock. I gave myself a pep talk and went for it.

"Cassidy, finish your homework so that you can take your bath." I issued this order before we even took our jackets off.

I marched upstairs and picked up a few toys from Cody's floor, walked into the bathroom and ran water for Cody's bath. Looking at the mountain of laundry I decided to sort the pile and wash as many loads as possible tonight and finish the rest Monday evening. I scooped up a load of clothes and ran them down the steps to place them in the washing machine. It made logical sense to clean out the dishwasher and spruce up the kitchen. After wiping down the countertops in the kitchen, I realized how bad the baseboards looked. The more I did around the house, the more I discovered other things that needed to be done. Whenever I knocked one chore down, five more sprouted up.

It dawned on me that the water was still running in the bathtub, so I ran upstairs and prayed that I did not create a bathroom flood. Luckily, I only had to slightly drain the water and I put Cody into the bath tub. I multi-tasked every multi-task. Stealing a moment from the clock, I sat on the toilet for a minute and just watched Cody splish and splash in the tub. My smile disguised my fatigue, and I washed him up and let him continue to play while putting on my gloves to clean the toilet. It didn't take long for me to dry him off, put on his pajamas, read a nursery rhyme, and say our bedtime prayers.

God must have pressed fast forward on my evening because when I checked the clock it was 8:30. All I knew at that point was the success of my evening all rested on rather or not my daughter had completed her language arts assignment. If the assignment was complete, she could take a bath for 15 minutes and there would be 15 minutes to spare, and when the dodo bird popped out I could stick out my tongue out and say, "so what if I'm rushing cuz I'm winning."

Making good of a trip down the steps, I chose another mound of dirty clothes to put into the washing machine.

"Cassidy, let me look over your assignment." There was no response. "Cassidy!" I prayed that I would find her stuffing her assignment into her backpack. I only saw Cassidy's legs sticking out of the bed. "Cassidy, what are you doing?"

"Momma, I'm looking for my homework."

"So for the last hour and a half you have been looking for your homework?"

I walked into the living room and saw an episode of iCarly playing on the television.

"You were watching TV. That's what you were doing." She looked apologetic, but she did not give a damn while she was watching TV. As a matter of fact, I already knew that she spent five minutes looking for the homework sheet and the rest of the time was spent watching television and listening for my footsteps.

I walked down the hallway in a zone that only mommas with the letters *A S* at the end are aware of. I don't think mommies with *I E S* have to go through this shit. I begin my own quest for her worksheet. I looked in the backpack, and I found a stack of sheets from every subject. Blank sheets of notebook paper, half folded school invitations, and two balled up notes that were sent home as parent notices for missing assignments. All of these papers were lightly crusted with Cheetos dust and smashed cookies. One by one I searched the stack of 70 random papers, and all I could think about was the time. I heard Super Mario Brothers 60-second countdown music playing in my head. My heart was not beating faster, but my daughter's heart raced because she knew that I had found the parent notices. While she was academically lazy, she had good common sense and she knew that if I found the assignment she was going to get a whoopin, and if I didn't find the assignment, she was going to get a whoopin.

"Which assignment is it again, language arts?"

"Yes."

"Is this it?" I produced a paper with the headline "The Life of a Pioneer" and rolled my eyes.

"Yes that's it!" her eyes brightened then dimmed.

My expression went blank. If I spanked her like I wanted to, it would make it harder for her to complete her assignment, so I resisted the urge to go for my belt. Besides, spanking her then would have only temporarily relieved my frustration, but it would have done very little for her motivation.

"Go to the table, turn that damn TV off, and finish this assignment," I growled while looking directly into Cassidy's eyes, hoping that by intimidating her, she would avoid this situation in the future. Cassidy didn't know if executing my last orders would save her ass, but I'm sure that she prayed a small prayer to God that it would cease the ass whoopin fire, and she went straight to the table.

Now, the clock struck 9:00, and the dodo bird said nine times, "You are always rushing." The original time table for the evening was a failure, so I mentally rearranged the time I had left on the clock. Cassidy's homework would take her 20 minutes to finish, and she would be bathed and asleep by quarter to 10:00. I began to prep for the morning shuffle.

I couldn't afford to waste any time, so while Cassidy finished her assignment I pulled out all of our clothes, ironed them and laid them out. There was nothing worse than having to hunt down socks or stockings in the morning. Twenty minutes had passed, and I collected a load of laundry to carry downstairs. Although my time parameters were not a success, I felt good about only having one more load of laundry to wash.

I saw Cassidy looking quizzically at the assignment...Ahhww shit... She is not finished with this assignment. I searched deep within my soul to find a soft spot to approach her questions or concerns. This moment was crucial and the wrong move on her part or mine could make this a nuclear situation. The tone of my voice was light and raspy. I hung on to each consonant at the end of each word. Just as my mother did before she whooped my ass many years ago.

"Cassidy are you finished?" No, well almost I just didn't understand how to answer this last question. The last question was a compare and contrast question.

"Well in order to compare and contrast this question, give examples of how it is the same and how it is different." I simplified the essence of the question and was confident that my explanation was easy enough for her to move along.

She replied with conviction. "Well that's not what my teacher said."

Oh hell no. No she did not pull the "that's not what my teacher said, and it is almost 10 o'clock.

"Well Cassidy, do it my way in the interest of time."

My patience was stretched as thin as pulled taffy, and I could hear the rhythm of the battle hymn of the baby momma beating louder and louder. Cassidy responded to the rhythm and finished her assignment as I instructed. At a quarter after 10 o'clock, I held on to my weekend marriage with Ryan so tightly, praying that I wouldn't be the only one making sure Cody's school work got finished or his room is cleaned. I get tired of I...I...I... and me...me...me. A little us, we, and he would sure be nice.

Finally, my race with time was over. I laid on my bed and reflected on my day. "That nigga had an empty condom box in his drawer." I said to myself in disbelief. I didn't have the time nor emotional energy to believe it. I dialed his number as I usually did at the end of night.

"Hey babe, what's up?" My voice was auto-tuned with energy.

"Shit, nothing, I just finished cleaning up my house."

"Oh, did you clean up your bedroom." The frequency of my voice changed for energetic to dry as hell.

"Nahh, I didn't even get to that part of the house." His words walked down an unmarked lane.

"Well, you need to at least clean out the drawer with the condom box in it." I wrapped the sentence in one breath.

"Oh shit, here we go." He responded dry and emotionless. "I wish you would not go into my drawers and snoop in my shit. I know that you are thinking that I had some girl in the house and was having sex. I know you think I was cheating, but that's not the case. I. Just. Wish. You. Would. Stay. Out. My. Shit."

Stewing in the power of silence, I held my peace. I pinched my lips together. My already small eyes pulled closer together, and I stopped breathing a little so that I could hear every syllable of his explanation.

"We just started getting our relationship back on track, and I really want you to trust me and please trust me on this one."

The bowels of a politician did not have Ryan's guts. I refrained from any type of verbal response and my brain tried to formulate what he would say next. *It was left by one of his boys or his cousins, or the condom box had been in his drawer for years, and he just never threw it away.* Then he started to tell me the true story.

"I don't like to get cum on my hands when I jack off, so I use condoms. I know that's hard to believe, but that is what happened and I don't want to lose my family over this." Obviously, I had been cheated on, but I didn't want to cheat myself out of a good laugh. So, I bugged up, cracked up, and laughed for 30 seconds.

"You want me to believe that you use condoms to jack off?"

"I want you to believe the truth, and that is the truth."

"So while you were at Walgreen's Ryan, shopping for toothpaste and lotion, you said to yourself, let me get some condoms because I am going to jack off later, and I don't want to get the shit on my hands? Oh, OK. Just stop it. Look, I have a long day tomorrow, and if that's what you said happened, that's what happened. I didn't find a pussy next to the box, so I expected you to have some kind of story, but this is classic Ryan."

"Now, you are just being sarcastic, I knew that you were not going to believe me, so now what?"

Check.

I asked myself what would be my next move. I didn't believe a fraction of his story, but if I told him that he was a liar, there would have to be some type of consequence. If I said that I believed him, I could sweep this under the rug and try and pretend that it never happened. I chose the latter.

"Ryan, that's a stretch. You are asking me to believe that you jack off with condoms, and I am having a hard time adding this story up, but if that is what you say happened then, OK."

"I love you Jazzmine, and I want this to work. Trust me."

"Alright." I replied hastily just to end the conversation and try to forget the entire ordeal as quickly as possible. I went to sleep with a heavy conscience and lightened the load by promising myself to leave Ryan's ass the next time I had to accept a lie. The trust of our relationship was tangled with so many lies. Is it a lie when Ryan says, "He wants our family to work?" We don't even live in the same house. Is it a lie, when Ryan says, "I love you?" Our son is almost two years old, and he's never asked me to marry him. Is it true that he can't afford a ring? I know that he has plenty of money in his bank account. I think I may need a bigger rug.

Inner City Blues

AT 6 AM my morning ritual begins. The alarm goes off. I press the snooze button three times, and at around 6:30, I finally get my day started. Giving myself 40 minutes to get dressed, get Cody dressed and Cassidy. A more reasonable approach would be for me to give myself at least an hour to get ready in the morning at the very least, but I always seem to go for the challenge instead of the Zen approach. However, I am Zen curious. I fantasize about running in the morning and drinking coffee while perusing work emails before 6 a.m. For now, those are all only ideas that run through my head as I press the snooze button. Using the Lord's divine intervention every morning just to get the kids dressed and off to school is certainly a miss management of divinity, but I employ it daily.

In the era before crack cocaine, my daughter would have been able to walk to the Catholic school around the corner from our home. It was only a few blocks away and it was a two minute car ride. I dropped my daughter off for school every morning at 7:15, and she ate breakfast at school. Cody ate breakfast at daycare.

"Bye Cassidy, don't forget to bring home your homework. Have a good day."

"Bye Mommy."

I kissed her goodbye and headed towards my next destination. While Cody kept himself occupied with a toy, I called Erin, my best friend since high school, college roommate, and professional colleague. To sum up our friendship, Erin and I could never fall out. She knows too much.

"Hey Girl." My morning voice had used up all of its powers to get my kids out of the door and my ready-for-the-world voice was in full effect.

"Hola Chica. You want to meet up for coffee in territory?"

"Girl, I will take a rain check. I will be having coffee with my manager this morning."

"I didn't know you had a ride-a-long today. Maybe we will hook up later in the week. How was your weekend?"

"It was Ok. I am just getting tired of that weekend shit with Ryan. I'm done with it bestie."

"You are leaving Ryan?"

"No, I am not done with the relationship. I am just done with going over there on the weekends. That is some stupid ass shit. I can't keep packing up my kids and visiting Ryan on the weekends. It just does not make sense for the family to visit daddy on the weekends."

"Well J, you have a point."

"How are you? Are you still having trouble keeping food down?"

"I have not been able to eat anything except Ted Drew's ice cream. I can't wait until this pregnancy thing is over."

"I know you can't. Well, girl let me get off this phone and drop Cody off at the daycare."

"Later Lady." Erin hung up the phone abruptly.

I decided to spare her and the world of the condom saga. I did not need a second or third opinion to determine the validity of the condom fable. Besides, Erin was riding high on her recent marital engagement, and I did not want to deflate our conversation with nonsense. More importantly, I did not want to lose any soul sistah cred for not chucking Ryan the deuces.

I exited on Shreve and made a left onto Sacramento. These streets mean nothing in the grand scheme of the United States of America. They are however, relevant in St. Louis because these streets border the epicenter of crime. One would think that a person with a decent income would not use a home daycare anywhere near a crime epicenter, but I have a unique St. Louis heritage. I haven't successfully traced my roots back to Africa, but I can say for certain that my ancestors are from the Carr Square Village Projects and my family members are here, bordering the epicenter of crime and in the eye of the storm. Your nice suit and education is a vehicle to your good job but your heart wants to relax and retreat somewhere that smells like fried pork chops and motor oil. I needed to walk up a few concrete steps and open up the door and hear somebody say......

"Hey Jazz."

"Hey Jennifer, how was your weekend?"

"Good Sweetie, I need to talk to you."

"What?"

"Cody bit Michael."

Michael was one of the older boys at the daycare, so I was hoping that his biting was a matter of self-defense and not a random act of vampirism.

"Was Michael doing anything to Cody?"

"Well, he had a toy and Cody wanted the toy, so he bit him."

"Did you punish Cody?"

"Yes, I put him in timeout. It's really no big deal. I have it under control. I just wanted to tell you that's all."

I left the daycare center feeling embarrassingly proud of the fact that my boy wanted a toy and was willing to fight for it. This feeling was short lived when I looked at the teddy bear shrine on the light post. I was humbled and reminded of the risk and the measures that black boys used to fight for the toys that they wanted from other black boys. A teddy bear shrine in St. Louis mostly marks the death of a black person under the age of 25 and usually it is a young man or boy. It is the 21st century version of a noose hanging from a tree. Only a mob of white men are not to blame. Whenever you see 40 teddy bears tied to a tree or light post or a stop sign, a black boy has been killed by another black boy, maybe a neighbor, a classmate, or a petty rival. Whenever I see 10 teddy bears tied to a light post, I get a little scared. I have a black son. It breaks my heart to live in a time where our sons are the casualties of our son's battles.

You Must Learn

IN AN OFFICE situation your boss observes your work ethic on a daily basis, but when you work in a field territory, your boss only observes you a few times a quarter. These brief meetings create the perception of how well you are performing. That's not a big deal if only I could control the mood of the doctors and their patients. I checked my lipstick in the mirror and answered a phone call before I went into the restaurant.

"Hello."

"Hey Ma, what's up?" My work counterpart replied.

"Not much. I ride with Morgan today, and I am about to walk into the Bread Company." I genuinely liked Morgan as a person, but I hated ride-a-longs.

"Oh, make sure you use the new clinical study, I used that during my last ride-along I had some really good dialogue with the physicians in Highland and she loved it"

"Thanks Ty for the heads up. I will definitely use the new study."

"Well alright Ma, we will rap later. Have a good day with Morgan."

Having the pressure of making a good impression for my manager and not being able to control every outcome of the day created pressure on my nerves.

I walked into the restaurant and spotted Morgan typing on her laptop in a small booth. I ordered coffee and a breakfast sandwich and joined her at the table.

"Hey Jazzmine, how are you beautiful? Your skin is just so great that it makes me sick to my stomach. You will never get a wrinkle. Here, take one of mine." She laughed.

"Morgan, you are just so hard on yourself. If I had your body, I would be dangerous."

Morgan was rock star pretty with long deep brown hair. She imagined her face to have a million wrinkles on it just like people suffering from anorexia imagine themselves with rolls of fat. Her body was banging, and while I wrestled with my alarm clock at 6 am she would have ran five miles. She had a perfect black girl booty, but as a white girl, she spent countless hours a week in the gym trying to get rid of it. Her personality was marked with a Chelsea Lately sense of humor. She didn't have a forearm tattoo, but if she did, it would say bitches make the world go round not because she was a bitch, but she wanted the world to respect her as business women that would bite if provoked.

Our relationship as manager and employee had an unusual realness that is rare in corporate America. It could have something to do with my "IT" factor, or maybe it stemmed from the fact that we were both part of the same sorority not Delta Sigma Theta, Sorority, Inc. but the sorority of single motherhood. She's a superhero in her own right. She never makes excuses. She just gets shit done. We finished our coffee, and she sat in the passenger's seat while I drove to my first office of the day.

I walked into this office in Southern Illinois. I am usually the only African-American face in town. With the exception of the brown faces that they see escorted by the police as an imprisoned patient. The staff members are always friendly and most of the doctors are cordial, but I do have a few clients that are straight up unshaved ass-holes. I get paid extremely well, so at the end of the day, I find a way to cope with the assitudes by telling myself that the asshole doctors have Asperger's, and apparently, they did not take their medication on that given day.

With my manager, I usually felt like a novice corner boy trying to earn respect and build relationships on my block.

"Ok Jazzmine, the hot button is making sure you put the products in every customer's hand. If we see six customers today, the company wants to know how many times you actually put the product in the customer's hand."

Ignoring the absurdity of the corporate initiative, I knew that at the end of the day, I will be scored and ranked by this standard and this alone. So, I made this task my focus and set aside my actual grow the business tactics. I placed the product in every customer's hand except one physician who definitely had a bad flare up with his Asperger's. He walked towards me stopped at his computer and looked directly into my eyes. As soon as I said hello and pulled out my company clinical he put his index to his lips and said, "Shhhhhhh."

That motherfucker shhhhh'ed me in front of my manager. Know that if this was the Hodiamont track in North St. Louis, I could kill him for that, but it's not, so I opened my eyes bright like a Girl Scout who had just had the door slammed in her face after asking, "Would you like to buy some cookies?" I scanned my manager's face for feedback." She mouthed the word, "Asshole."

I said, "I know right." The staff members looked at me apologetically and I we went to the next doctor's station as if that scene never happened.

Collectively, the day went well. I earned my token status coins but not one power dollar. On the ride home we exchanged notes on who had the most arrogant boyfriend. Morgan's boyfriend was a handsome small town attorney who felt that he was God's gift to all women. To repay the Lord for his grace and mercy, he shared his time with Morgan. His idea of a special evening for Morgan was wherever he showed up, and if he was a little darker, I would have thought that he was the long lost brother of Ryan. I didn't dare mention the condom story but Morgan shared a story that involved her boyfriend and her babysitter. Niggaz come in all different shades even white. I dropped Morgan off at her car, and I began my journey back to the city. My drive home always started with a call to my best friend, Erin. I told her about my encounter with the aforementioned asshole doctor. She called him a bastard, and we changed the subject to a more pressing issue, my daughter and her homework.

"Cassidy needs to get it together."

"Girl, what she do now?"

"Apparently not enough in science, she had a D on her progress report. I taught biology and my child is getting a D in science. What the hell?"

"Yeah Jazz, I see how that pisses you off. Maybe she doesn't understand it."

"I would accept that, but I know that she doesn't even try. Let me call you right back. This is Cassidy's school on the other line." I took a deep breath and held it in my chest. I exhaled and rolled my eyes as I said, "hello."

"Good evening Ms. Steele, this is Mrs. Crow the principal of St. Francis, and I really would like to schedule a conference with you and Cassidy's teachers." I don't want you to be alarmed, but Cassidy is not turning in her homework assignments, and she is not focusing during class time. Parent teacher conferences are next month and I really think we should meet before the conference. We need to nip this in the bud before she gets even farther behind."

"OK Mrs. Crow, I can make arrangements to be at the school tomorrow at 3:00."

"Sounds great, I look forward to meeting with you tomorrow."

Cassidy attended a small Catholic elementary school, and there was no way a child could fly under the radar. The entire fourth grade class had only 17 kids. Even though we were not Catholic, I chose a

Catholic school, simply because St. Louis Public Schools were barely accredited.

I called my mom to give me a parent pep talk. My mom is my personal trainer for motherhood and listening to her talk sounds a lot like advice that Roger Mayweather gives to Floyd in between boxing rounds.

"Momma, I don't know what to do with Cassidy. I am tired of her teachers calling me and telling me that Cassidy is not turning in her homework assignments. I am not spending all of this money on private school education so she can just wear a plaid skirt. She is not doing her homework, and it's embarrassing. I don't know what else to do."

"Shit, that's your fault." My mom replied in a matter of fact tone.

"How is it my fault? When she comes home it's peaceful. Her room is decorated the way she wanted it. She does not go to bed hungry. Dinner is always hot and ready. We go on nice vacations. She has more toys than a toy store."

"Every day I ask her did she finish her homework and she tells me she doesn't have any. So please help me understand how I am not doing my job?" My mom's voice became quiet and serious.

"You.... Ask..... Her. And she is fucking lying to you. Stop asking her. Don't ask her another motherfuckin time if she has homework or if she finished it. Cuz she's lyin and playin the shit out of you. See your ass is too soft. You need to toughen up. Make that ass show you her finished homework each and every night, but don't take her word for it. That makes you the damn fool. You too damn soft. You need to start letting Cassidy know who run it, or else Cassidy is going to continue to half ass do her work in school, and not do her homework and those teachers, will continue to call you. I have to tell the parents of my students all the time to stop asking their kids things and start telling them what to do."

"You're right mom. I just don't understand why Cassidy is so unmotivated."

"Stop trying to understand. Motivate that ass with a belt."

I am not against spanking my children, and if I could beat intellectual brilliance into my child, I would. If my education woes with my daughter could be solved by a belt, immediately following a healthy dinner, I would start swinging my belt around like Pooty Tang. Is that the secret to the math aptitude of Asian students? Are Indian kids getting a swift kick in their behinds by their parents to encourage and foster an interest in computers? Probably not. My mom made some valid points and the bottom line is that I have to change my ways. I wish she was only five ass whoopins away from the honor roll, but there is a difference between discipline and punishment. I want her to love learning and be driven to compete with her brightest classmates. Unfortunately, promises of neither rewards nor punishments are working, so imma try something new.

Wildflower

MY WORK DAY began smoothly and ended predictably. I looked into the mirror on my sun visor, and my makeup even looked neater and relaxed. After a long day of working and driving I picked up Cody from daycare. On my way to Cassidy's school, I called Cassidy's dad. He lived in Nashville and was a better father when we lived in Nashville. Sometimes, I think he forgets he has a child now that we are in St. Louis. I dialed his number. The phone rang and went to voicemail. We hadn't heard from him in two months, and I wanted to ask him if he would be able to make it to St. Louis for Cassidy's birthday weekend. Chris never checked his voicemail messages, so leaving a message was pointless, and every time I called him, it would piss me off. Anything could happen, and I would not be able to dial him directly. *He is too old for this shit.*

When I taught school in Nashville, his checks came on time, and he spent time with Cassidy. It was not until I turned corporate that he went milk carton missing. In the summers, Cassidy would tell him about how we cruised to Mexico or canoed in the Pocono Mountains. I knew that Chris struggled financially. He had three kids and his girl was a stay at home mom. Whenever we talked, I never made the conversations about the back child support. Cassidy and Chris's time together was not a jet setting affair, but she would trade in the mountains and Mexico any day to spend a week with her brothers and sister in Nashville. Maybe he felt that she didn't need him anymore. I really didn't know what his problem was but he bettah pick up the motherfuckin phone. Whew, I need to change my head movie; my Cooleyitis is started to flare up.

I pulled into the school and parked near the playground area were the kids played when the weather permitted. After signing Cassidy out of aftercare, she immediately asked.

"So, what's for dinner?"

"Well, I don't get a hello, how was your day mother, I love you or nothing?"

"Hello. How was your day mother? I love you. What's for dinner?" She replied in a robotic tweenish manner.

"We knocked off the lasagna last night. I don't feel like cooking, so you choose."

"Sweetie Pies." Her eyes lit up and so did mine.

I could go for Sweetie Pies, and I knew that she would say that. My daughter wasn't big on fast food, and I was happy we were on the same page. We pulled up to Sweetie Pies and were greeted by a man with a light complexion and a happy golden tooth grin. Every time, I saw this man, I thought to myself that he must be one of the happiest people on the planet. I never saw a man refill an orange soda and grab a bottle of hot sauce with so much pride. Working at Sweetie Pies was more than just a job for him. He operated as if he was a part of something big. I saw him leaving the restaurant pushing the shit out of his short dog Cadillac. Nobody could tell this man nothing.

I picked up Cody and propped him on my hip while we walked down the line and made our dinner selections from the steam table. I adjusted my shirt collar and pulled down my gray suit jacket.

"For here or to go?" A brown skinned woman with a hairnet and extra-long false eyelashes asked as soon as we made eye contact.

"For here. I will have the fried chicken dinner." I said in one breath to keep with the rhythm of the line.

THE SHO NUFF BLUES

"Ok, wait one second; some fresh chicken is comin out."

I was a regular in the line, and I always got fresh chicken and peach cobbler crust love. She plated my yams and macaroni and stuffed my crusty peach cobbler in a to-go container for later. At the end of the line, a seasoned lady with brown skin and a serious face collected my money and a bright smile appeared from nowhere.

"So how was your day?" The generic question rolled off of my tongue effortlessly.

"It was good." All of her days were good. This was my daughter's auto-generated response.

"Well, what made it good?"

"We got to play outside during lunch."

Cassidy's school was once a dormitory for nuns. The playground consisted of a blacktop that moonlighted as a parking lot in the evenings. I didn't send her to the school because of the awesome playground, and despite not having any playground equipment, playing outside made Cassidy's day.

"What did you do outside?"

"It was crazy mom. My friend, Olivia, married a grape."

"What did you say?" Cassidy could tell by the look on my face that she had to explain the ceremony in detail.

"You heard me mom. Olivia married a grape, and then someone smashed the grape and killed it."

"O...K... uhh how did Olivia handle the loss of her beloved grape?"

"She had a funeral for the grape."

"Of course she did." I replied. "Did anyone attend the funeral?"

"Yes, I attended the funeral, Nisha, Ciara and a few of my other friends."

"So let me get this straight, you went to a funeral for a grape?"

"Yes, yes I did." She squeezed her laughter in between her cheeks to hold it in.

"My poor baby needs a slide and a swing. You and your friends are losing your minds. No one can say that you don't use your

imagination." I continued to probe my daughter for details surrounding the marriage and death of Olivia's beloved grape then changed
the topic to Cassidy's upcoming birthday.

"Cassidy, I know that you usually have a large birthday party, but
this year you have not earned it. I enjoy having birthday parties for
you, but this year we are going to do something really small. When
we go to Nashville for TSU's homecoming in November, your dad will
have a party for you as long as you bring your grades up." Her eyes
were sad when I talked about downsizing her party, and they livened
up a bit after I mentioned her dad. The sad part about the conversation was that the part about her dad's reward was as counterfeit as
Santa Clause and his elves.   I wish my daughter's first series of dis-
appointments from a man didn't come from her dad, but it was too
late and out of my control. I also wish that her mind could remain
innocent, carefree and fixed on the death of a grape instead of the
absence of her father.

While talking with Cassidy, I missed the mess that Cody made
with the sugar and macaroni and cheese.

"Cody, why did you do that?"

"More please." Was his response and he pointed to the sugar. The
floor was full of sugar and other objects that Cody decided were better off on the floor. I stooped down to try and clean up Cody's grand
mess. As I looked up I saw Miss Robbie. She grabbed Cody's hand and
took a seat next to Cassidy.

Miss Robbie was the owner of Sweetie Pies. Her beauty was time-
less and ageless. Her hair was hidden under a net, and her makeup
was always flawless. Whenever, I came to Sweetie Pies, Miss Robbie
was working, and I don't know how she did it, but she managed to cook
in the hot kitchen, without breaking a sweat. I never saw her mascara
run and her lipstick was always its true original color. Whenever I
cooked Sunday dinner for more than five people, I would look like I
had just had a fight and lost. I would clean up before my company
would arrive, but the behind the scene show was not a good look.

"This is the owner of the restaurant, Cassidy." I made sure that my daughter knew that a woman ran the Sweetie Pie operation.

"I know mom. We met her last time."

"Ahhw look at this handsome little one." She smiled at Cody and he smiled back. "And you are a pretty girl." She looked at Cassidy who gave a shy grin.

"Thanks, they keep me busy."

"I am sure they do, and they keep me busy around this place. Well, I have some food to cook, thanks for stopping by."

I nodded and smiled as a gesture goodbye and our eyes had their own salutation.

Miss Robbie's eyes told my eyes, "Just because life isn't perfect doesn't mean that it can't be amazing, have a good evening."

I was so tired and sluggish, and I thought I could easily slip into a carb coma. Somehow I made it home.

"Cassidy, where is your book bag?"

"Here."

I checked Cassidy's school agenda and opened up to today's date. The assignment columns were blank, and I knew that she had homework.

"Where is your homework?" Cassidy produced a few handouts. "Have a seat at the table. Turn the television off, and finish your homework."

I was practicing my mom's militant tactics and stayed close to the kitchen table area so that I could monitor Cassidy's focus. One hour later, Cassidy's homework was complete. Cody redecorated the living room floor with his toys and was playing a game that only he understood. After bath time, play time, and cleaning time, the time was now 9 o'clock. After story time and prayer time, the time was now 9:20, and it was finally my time.

I exhaled and enjoyed the stillness of my bedroom. I found entertainment in the shade of paint on my bedroom wall. I was exhausted and did not have the energy for anything else. Parenting is a two-man sport. When you play it solo you get tiyad…not tired or fatigued but tiyad. I only sit down when I'm eating. All my other time in the evening is accounted for. Occasionally, I try and steal a few minutes from my schedule but guilt and chores pile up making the stolen moments unworthy. Housewives would slit their wrists, if they had to play my hand. I once overheard a pair of housewives chatting over lattes at Starbucks.

"Beth, how is everything going?"

"Everything is fine now, but I'm not sure how I will get through the holidays."

"What's going on?"

"Ben's travel schedule for work is going to be ridiculous in November and half of the month in December. I will be home with the kids alone. We entertain for the holidays, and I will be like a single mother for almost six weeks. My life is going to be crazy."

There I sat at the table beside her, a true single mother. While working on my lunch break, I didn't have the luxury to consider my Thanksgiving or Christmas schedule. I wanted to go to the table and say, "Excuse me, will the household bills still come in Ben's name while he is traveling for work?" And before she would answer, I would stare her in the eye and say, "Fuck your latte," knock it on the ground and walk away.

Ryan played basketball for the church league on Tuesdays and Thursdays and because his games are in the city. It's more convenient for him to stay in the city instead of taking the one hour hike back to his home. So Tuesday and Thursday nights are his dedicated family time evenings. After a quick shower, I put on a set of sexy yet comfortable pajamas and waited for his knock. The knock came and I used energy from a special tank to gallop down the stairs and open the front door.

"Hey," I smiled and leaned in to kiss him lightly on his lips.

"Hey Mamma,"

I headed upstairs and Ryan felt on my booty like a 13-year-old boy playing catch-a-girl-get-a-girl. I channel surfed while he showered. Ten minutes later, he came into my room with his towel wrapped around his waist. Just above his waist and on the sides of his body, I could see every line in his abdomen muscles. He dropped the towel and put on a pair of hoop shorts.

"I need to check out my boy."

"He's asleep."

"I know. I just like looking at him."

He went into our son's room and smiled at his sleeping face. I didn't see the look on this particular day, but I have seen it. It's the same look in his eyes that he gets when he looks at a luxury car, or a mansion and the same look that he used to give me when we first met.

"How was your day sweetheart?" He propped two pillows behind his head, grabbed the remote and changed the television to ESPN.

"It was long. I am exhausted."

"I know you are. Driving around all day in your free car with your free gas and talking to doctors all day would drain anybody." He replied sarcastically.

"Whatever Ryan, you are trying to be funny. Working and driving all day and taking care of kids in the evening drains you."

"No, pouring asphalt and tarring roofs during hot summer days drains you. Pulling mobile homes on a truck through narrow country roads drains you. You don't know how good you have it."

"You act like I live a life of leisure. I am a full time employee and a full time mom."

"Look, I take care of my part; I already told you Cody can live with me until we get married. That way you wouldn't have so much on you in the evenings, and you can focus on getting Cassidy on track in school."

"Don't do me any motherfucking favors." I barked.

"You get so sensitive; I didn't mean it like that. I just don't want you to be stressed out. That's all. I want you to know that I am here to support you. I'm sorry if it came out the wrong way."

He channel surfed until he found a show that we both could laugh at and the mood was lightened. We took an hour nap, and I woke up with my butt being poked by Ryan's you know what. I played the role of a happily married woman for about thirty minutes. A real married woman would have had a headache for sure on this night. Ryan didn't help with the kids. He didn't help with chores or dinner. I bet those latte ladies would not have given it up tonight, but I did.

My love for Ryan was a chitterling type of love. It wasn't the best part of the pig. In fact it's the part with all the shit in it, but when you clean it up and season it right, you can learn to acquire a taste for it. It's detestable by most, enjoyed by few, but when that's all you got, you learn to make do.

I Wish

I **WAS SIX** weeks clean of my weekend trips to Ryan's, and my new routine started paying off. I felt renewed, and I even flirted with the possibility of exercising. Cassidy's school did not call me every day or send notes home for missing assignments. I was finally establishing order and stability in my home. The cinnamon and pumpkin colored leaves on the trees painted a scene of tranquility and peace, and I took a moment to recognize them as I drove through the long road to Hardin, IL. I traveled miles and miles a day to see my clients, but when I focused on the scene and not the distance, it made the time pass by with ease. The friendly small town spirited clients, made the journey worth my while. I drove into an unpaved lot covered with rocks and walked into a doctor's office with one of the best views in America. The office sat on the banks of the Mississippi River and the trees sported every shade of fall that an artist could ever paint. Out of the corner of my eye, I spotted a white elderly couple looking at me suspiciously. They pretended not to look at me, and I pretended that I didn't notice them. I carried bags of red lobster into the office just in time for my lunch appointment.

"Well, hi there stranger." Doc closed the book titled *Common Sense* by Glenn Beck and removed his glasses and gave me a warm smile.

"Hello. It feels like I've been missed." Doc was one of my favorite clients. He was a family man from his skin to his core.

"Thanks for bringing us Red Lobster. It's our favorite." One of the staff members said.

"So, what's new?" The doctor asked the question that every pharmaceutical sales professional hears at every sales workshop.

"Nothing on my end. I was hoping that you could tell me about a new patient that you prescribed my product to." Boom, I threw the ball back to him.

He smiled and said, "I haven't prescribed your product yet, but I will just keep reminding me." My smile remained innocent, but my mind went into my babies need new pairs of shoes mode.

"Now doctor that is the same answer you gave me last time." I batted my eyes and gave him a look like a Girl Scout that was struggling to sell her last case of short bread cookies.

I pulled out a clinical study. Then it started to happen.

"We agreed that most of your patients had weight to lose. I showed you the outcomes from the study that proved that this medication would assist your patients in losing weight. Do you recall our last conversation?" My head started shifting from left to right and the doctor noticed.

"Did you just move your head from side to side?" He asked with one breath infused with laughter.

"Yes doctor, this is serious, and the head sway is a natural reflex."

"That's funny. You have to forgive me, but I'm from Hardin, and we didn't have any African-Americans around when I was in school, and we don't have very many around today. I have seen African-Americans sway their necks on television, but I didn't know that was real." The small staff of three all started to giggle.

"Well doctor it is real, and you need to find a real patient to prescribe my products for and not just because I sway my neck, but because it's a safe and efficacious product." My neck continued to sway and the receptionist chimed in.

"The neck roll is priceless; we don't see that every day."

"Angie, I'm sure you do something similar when you mean business, you probably give someone the eye." And I changed my facial expression to model an example of the eye.

"Oh, yes I sure do and nobody wants me to give them the eye." She gave me a brief snapshot of the eye.

"If looks could kill, I would be dead."

"How are the kiddos?" Angie asked.

"The kids are fine. We are going on a cruise with my mom's side of the family and Cassidy is so excited.

"Are you taking your son?"

"No, I don't think he is old enough to remember or appreciate it. He will miss this one."

"Who will he stay with, while you guys are cruising?" She asked curiously.

"With his dad." I wished I could check my face in the mirror to make sure that it didn't have the getoutofmydamnbusiness look on it.

"Oh so he will get some major daddy points."

"He will get a few, but his account is full of daddy points." I looked up at the clock, "Is it 1:30 already? I have to get on the road. Happy Friday! See you guys next time." I left the office looking happier than I did when I walked through the door. I was not numb to feeling ashamed of being unmarried with children. I have just mastered the emotional art of crying without tears and smiling at the same time.

I got back into my car and returned a missed call from my Grandmother.

"Hey Granny."

"Hey Jazz, did you get my message?"

"No, I haven't checked them yet. What's up?"

"Not much. Granny just ain't been feeling well lately, but something came over me, and I cleaned and picked some greens, and I wanted to let you know that they will be ready on Sunday."

"I will be in the building, what would you like for me to bring?"

"Oh just bring whatever.   Phyllis is frying some chicken and making the macaroni and cheese. I am going to call Lamonia and ask her
to make the sweet potato casserole. You can bake something sweet
if you are up to it. I know its last minute and you're busy so don't
worry yourself over it."

"I saw a recipe in Southern Living for a sour cream iced lemon
pound cake. I will make it and bring it over."

"Oh sounds good. I used to make an iced lemon pound cake."

"I remember. That is why I clipped it from the magazine."

"I'm going to get off this phone. When Granny talks too long, I
start losing my breath."

"Alright Granny. Don't try and get old on me."

"Chile it's too late. See you on Sunday. Love ya."

When I was a child, my grandmother cooked every Sunday, and
we feasted on fried chicken, greens, macaroni and cheese, candied
yams, and buttermilk cornbread as if it was recommended by the
surgeon general himself. Now, that my grandmother is getting
older she doesn't cook as much and when she does, and we get
the call, it is a holiday.   I have learned and mastered most of my
grandmother's recipes.   I was trained in the kitchen personally
by Granny herself. However, if you put the food that I have prepared against the food that she has prepared, Granny would win,
hands down. Maybe it's because she is a better cook or maybe it's
because she has not given me all of the ingredients in the recipes.
I always tease my grandmother and say, "Granny, if you are trying
to get into heaven, it's about time you come clean with the real
cornbread recipe."

I was hype the rest of the day. I was doing the my-granny-is-mak-
ing-greens dance in my car. I saw a few more clients and shut the
work day down. It's the Week Ennnnnnnnd Baby!

Friday flashed by. Saturday zoomed away, and Sunday moved at
a slow pace. Joel Osteen talked while I drank my coffee and folded
clothes. I agreed a few times with some statements that he made,

said Amen a few times and decided to play church hooky and stay home. My relationship with God was solid enough to know that this did not count as a full day of worshipping the Lord, and my prayer was that it would count for something. It mattered to me. I received a word at the First Baptist Couch of Christ.

While drinking my second cup of coffee, I put some turkey bacon in the microwave and made a batter for pancakes. After the scent of bacon floated in the air, magically my kids appeared in the living room and started watching cartoons. I watched that moment like I watched the trees in Hardin and honored the view from my kitchen. I turned my head to put the eggs back into the refrigerator and I heard crying.

"Cassidy, what happened?" I needed an explanation as to why my kids were messing with my energy, my chi.

"Cody hit me in the head with a bat."

I saw guilt painted all over his face, and he went to his sister, kissed her, and said sorry in the most adorable two-year-old boy voice that a person could ever hear. Cassidy was unsatisfied with his apology, and I was confused. I needed to show Cassidy that I was on her side and not transfixed with Cody's charm. I told him to go to the corner, and he was pissed. Mommy mission complete!

We chilled and relaxed and relaxed and chilled some more until it was time to go to Granny's house. She lived about 30 minutes from the city, in the suburbs of St. Louis. I crossed the same bridge that I crossed to visit Ryan and I was remarkably proud of the weekends that I had not spent at his home. I never told him that I was not going to come over his house on the weekends anymore. *I can show him better than I can tell him.*

"Where we goin mom?"

"Crazy." I said with a smile

"For real mom, I'm hungry. Can we stop and get something to eat?" I ignored her and kept driving.

"Mommy, I'm hungry."

"Hi Hungry, I'm mommy. How are you?" Cassidy rolled her eyes. She knew that I could keep this up for at least 10 minutes. Cody didn't really understand the conversation, but he joined in.

"I'm hungry." He said it clearly, and I could tell by the way he looked at me that he was waiting for my response.

"Hi, Hungry, I'm mommy. How are you?" He busted out laughing, and we all joined in. We had a brief chat about the upcoming week's events and arrived at our destination.

I parked my car behind my brother's Dodge pickup truck. I opened the door, and the aroma from Granny's kitchen met me at the curb. The scent of meat cooking from Granny's kitchen and the smell of Bounce dryer sheets from the laundry reminded me of my childhood and I floated in the direction of the door. I took a roll call of the people who were already there. I saw my daddy's truck. Lamonia was here. Jay and his family, uncle Kevin, my aunt Phyllis's van, and my cousin Brittany's car was parked in front of me. My cousin Keisha's car was parked near my cousin Phillip's vehicle. I saw a rental car in the driveway that must have belonged to someone from out of town. There were ten cars strategically parked in front of and near my grandmother's 1,000 square foot villa.

I carried in my plastic container holding my pound cake and Cody insisted on walking up the hill without the assistance of Cassidy or me. I turned the doorknob and walked into my favorite audience, my family. Everyone smiled as we walked through the door.

"Hey Jazz, whatcha got?" Lamonia said first.

My second mother, Lisa, smiled and said, "Ahhww look at my black little Miss Martha Stewart.

"This is what grown people do." I smiled and kissed and hugged each and everyone in the small kitchen. After I made my rounds, I looked around and my kids swam to the basement and jumped into the sea of playing children.

"Is the food ready?" It was already 6 o'clock in the evening, but I didn't see any dirty plates on the table.

"Everything except the corn bread, Jazz. You feel like making the corn bread?" My grandmother asked, and I wouldn't dare say no. I didn't want to make the cornbread. Not because I didn't feel like it but because I was intimidated by being in the same kitchen with my grandmother. I cooked all the time in my own kitchen, but I didn't feel worthy in hers.

"Yes, Granny, I will do it." I accepted the responsibility, and there were a thousand eyes on me. My grandmother's kitchen was small and unorganized, and I had to hunt for every utensil and ingredient.

"Granny, where is the flour?"

"Look in the pantry, or look behind the sack of potatoes in the lower cabinet."

"Where is the iron skillet?"

"Go in the garage. Look to your left. It should be on the shelf were the pots are." She started to look frustrated and impatient. Of course, I should have known that the iron skillet was located in the garage. Is that not where most people keep their iron skillets?

After winning the cornbread ingredient scavenger hunt, I finally had all of the ingredients, and it was time to start cracking some eggs and mixing the ingredients together. I felt my grandmother's eyes analyzing my techniques.

"You don't mix your dry ingredients together before you add the wet ones?"

"I did that already Granny." I said it as if I was only a few years older than my son and younger than my daughter.

"Oh, well I don't think you mixed it good enough. I don't know how your bread is going to turn out, but we will see. "

"She don't know what she's doing, Granny. Jay should have made the cornbread. He made it last time." My younger cousin, Brittany, said.

"Look, I don't need no comments from the peanut gallery, lil girl. I got this." I smiled and prayed that my cornbread would come out right. My family saw the frustration in my face, and they all decided to take jabs at me. It was all in good humor, but the jabs came one after the other.

"She tryin to be too cute with it," said my Uncle Kevin.

"It's a good thing that I don't eat cornbread," said Stacy.

"Did you let the oil get hot in the oven before you put the batter in the skillet?" I knew Lamonia would have something to say. Then, I shut the madness down.

"Now wait one minute. Everybody that is watching could have made the cornbread. Imma need this live audience to get real quiet until my cornbread is ready. I know what I am doing, OK."

My dad laughed at the site of me trying to get everybody to take me serious. I poked out my lips and narrowed my eyes. In reality everybody saw me more like a Lucille Ball than Moms Mabley.

Thirty five minutes later, my grandmother took the first bite of my cornbread and everyone watched her reaction. "Not bad, Jazz. It tastes like my bread. I just have one suggestion. Let your oil in your skillet get a little hotter. That's how I make my edges crispy."

Every time I make cornbread in her kitchen she has a suggestion. If she would just give me the real recipe, I wouldn't have to go through this every time.

"Is Ryan going to come by? I made his favorite, ox tails?"

"Yes, he had to work, but he said that he would come later."

Ryan earned a special place in my grandmother's heart. Every time it snowed, he would make sure he shoveled her snow, and he was an excellent father to Cody. He got along with Cassidy fairly well. In reality, it was a small price to pay for a real estate plot of someone's heart, but my Grandmother had extremely low expectations of men, and any gesture counted for something. The only thing that my grandmother knew about her father was that he was Jewish and his family owned and operated the dry cleaner that her mother worked for. So any man that was present in their child's life was special. Ryan was on the special list, and I never talked her out of it. I listened to her advice on how to coach and scheme Ryan into marriage.

"When I married your grandfather, I was pregnant with your Aunt Lynn. I told him that we are going to get married. We went to the courthouse on his next day off work and got married. Afterwards, we ate hotdogs at the nearby diner, and we were married for over 40 years." I'd heard that story dozens of time. It made me laugh as a kid, but as an adult, it made me cry.

"So Granny, I'm just supposed to tell Ryan we are going to get married, pick a date, do it, and eat a hot dog?" *I don't even like hotdogs.* If she wanted to spoil Ryan with special meals as a bonus package to my already complete package, that was up to her, but I'm scaling back on my features. He's going to need my granny's ox tails and a new girl if he keeps pressing the snooze button on marriage.

We ate ourselves sick and as the food settled the conversations started to pick up again. Everyone in my family was a tableside philosopher. My cousin, Phillip, was the authority on pop culture. Lamonia pontificated on matters of love and Jay, my extremely opinionated, ultra-passionate, cantankerous cousin, would start off all of the political and religious conversations.

"So, I was at the barbershop and we was talking about what Obama has done for the black community since he's been in the White House. Gas prices and unemployment are high. People can't find jobs. Schools are still bad. I don't think he has done anything for the black community." Jay stood straight up in his chair and waited for a response.

Anytime the source of a datable issue came from the barber shop, I knew we were in for a long night. We spent hours around this table eating chicken and talking about Jay's barber shop debates regarding child support, divorce settlements, education, how to find a good wife, when to divorce your good wife, monogamy, polygamy, and so forth and so on. I hope Jay's barber has a degree in psychology because he has a hell of a platform, and he needs to make sure he is disseminating more than opinionated information but research based information. It's a good thing Cassidy had her homework complete and our clothes were ready for the next day, cuz the shit just got real.

"Those aren't black issues. Those are American issues," my dad retorted. "But it's worse for us, and he's a black president. Look at the statistics. Look at the statistics for black men who are unemployed. Look at the statistics for the schools in black communities.

"It has always been harder for blacks during rough times. These young boys now are making things harder for themselves. I interviewed three solid black candidates and decided to hire two of them. Neither of the candidates was cleared through my human resources department because of felonies on their records. I could tell that these were solid men that made stupid mistakes to sell drugs in their 20's, but it was nothing that I could do for them and Obama can't help them either." The self-accountability card was slammed on the table. This card could start a fight easier than it could start a revolution.

"How you think drugs are getting into the community? You think those men that you interviewed were able to bring drugs to St. Louis?" Jay's head nodded after every word that he spoke. If no one else agreed with him, it was all good because he had already agreed with himself a hundred times.

My second mom, Lisa, started making her way towards a blue cooler that one would assume was filled with soft drinks. She pulled out a large bottle of Grey Goose vodka, a large bottle of Malibu rum, and a variety of fruit juices. Magically, a large pitcher appeared on the kitchen counter, and she poured and stirred until her potion was complete. She took the final taste test. You knew that it was the final test because after she tasted from the spoon, smiled until her eyes disappeared, and did a little two-step, it was time to drink. She filled red Solo cups with the infamous Lisa Juice and the crowd started to separate. The debaters stayed in the kitchen, and the reality show watchers migrated to the living room. Everyone looked surprised when we heard a knock at the door. We never knock on Granny's door. We just walk right in, so we knew that it had to be Ryan.

"Hello. Hello. Hello. How is everyone doing?" Ryan greeted the room in a deep low tone and gave everyone a small cool smile.

"Hey Ryan," came from multiple mouths with tight smiles.

"Cody is something else. I don't know what you are going to do with that boy." Lamonia said while shaking her head as if there was a story behind her statement.

"My son is something else. He is something special. He is something great and for a small fee, I will let you babysit." Ryan intended to be humorous, but because of his my-shit-don't-stink persona it came across as an arrogant response.

"I'm just saying ya'll have something on ya'll hands," and she left the conversation alone.

Ryan walked past the reality show watchers, towards the kitchen, made a plate, and chimed in on the debate. Obama's presidential career was still under review and according to statements and arguments that were made at the table, Presidents Nixon, Carter, Reagan, and the Bushes were all responsible for the unemployed men that my dad could not hire. Obama and Clinton were not totally in the clear. They needed to do more to rectify the situation that the aforementioned presidents conspired to create. I couldn't take it anymore, and I listened for a calm moment in the conversation so I could interject.

"Those men had a choice. They didn't have to sell drugs."

"That's like putting candy in front of a baby's face and expecting them not to eat it. These men are underemployed and trying to hustle by any means necessary." My cousin Jay snapped at my remark and ironically used a Malcom X quote to support why black men are selling crack cocaine.

"They are not babies, Jay. They are men, and if they walk into every trap in the city, they will suffer the consequences." I asserted. The conversation did not have a place to elaborate on the traps of the city but it would be nice if they were as cool as Young Jeezy makes them out to be in his rap lyrics. If the city trap was a place where I could walk into and get rich and live like a rapper, I'd want to be on the guest list. Since it's the place where young men and young boys walk in to get rich and walk out poor felons that can't get employed in the kitchen of a bank, I think I will avoid it. Cody may be something else, but he will not be chanting, meet me at the Trap. I continued to make my point.

"Take crack off the streets and schools and employment would improve." I said it as if it could happen overnight. As if I lived in a world by which a few good men could knock on a few doors and say, "Are there any crack dealers or users here?" And the resident would say, "Yes sir, there are two crack dealers here." And the crack eradicator would say, "Well, turn it over buddies." The dealers would then hand over their pellets of crack and any unprocessed cocaine powder and the crack crusader would move to the next house and say, "Are there any crack dealers or users in the house?" A lady would come to the door and answer, "Why yes sir, I smoke crack." And the crack crusader would reply, "Well ma'am, could you stop? And the lady would politely say, "That sounds like a wonderful idea, I will stop this morning. Good day sir."

"You are in la la land, Jazz. That will never happen." My cousin snapped me back into reality. He may very well be right, and he could be wrong. Slavery in America lasted for over 400 years, and all throughout history there were African-Americans who tried to end it. Do you know how crazy slaves must have sounded to the other slaves in the 1700's when they talked about freedom? Crack has not even been around for 40 years. If I told my family right now during this conversation that I wanted to lead a movement to end the use and distribution of crack cocaine, would they tell me that my task would be easier or more difficult than Harriet Tubman's? Just a thought.

My dad ended the debate without a formal motion process. "Is it after 9 o'clock already? Lisa, tell Tyler, it's time to leave."

"Dad, I wanted to take Kalynn and Darian, to Tennessee State's Homecoming. It's two weekends away. Is it ok if they come?

"I don't have a problem with that." Kalynn and Darian were generally referred to as "the twins," and they were in their senior year of high school. Giving them a taste of college life at a historically black university was my responsibility as a big sister. We were all glad that our road trip received dad's stamp of approval.

"Get geeked. Get geeked. It's homecoming week." They both said in concert. They heard me say this at least a dozen times over the years, and by the time, we leave for Nashville they will know the entire chant.

Ryan migrated to my grandmother's room, where my Granny was resting. Ryan, myself and six of my cousins sat in my grandmother's room for another 30 minutes or so. We were not doing or saying much of anything, but we all hung around so that we didn't miss anything. Just in case something started to happen.

You Caint Play with My YoYo

TSU'S HOMECOMING WEEKEND should be a national holiday. The pep rally, the tea-less tea parties, the mixers, and the tailgating will never get old.   This year I played hostess to my siblings. The duo commonly referred to as "the twins" were going to get a glimpse of real collegiate life. Cassidy would spend the night with her best friend Nia, and I finally talked to Cassidy's dad, and he agreed to take the girls out for Cassidy's birthday on Saturday.   We left my house before sunrise. Cassidy and the twins fell asleep as soon as they situated themselves in the car, and I called Chris to tell him that we were on the road. I dialed his number and after the second ring, he answered. I couldn't believe it. I was in disbelief.

"Chris, what are doing up? I was expecting to leave you a message on your voicemail."

"I'm still working. I haven't slept in two days."

"What time are you picking up the girls tomorrow? I need to know so that I can let Kim know the plan." Kim was more like a sister to me than a friend and our daughters remained friends. We took turns helping each other untangle our lives and when the ball became too tricky to sort. We knew which parts to throw away and which parts to keep.

"I'm going to try and make it to Kim's, but I don't know what time."
His vocabulary was full of inconclusive answers.

"What do you mean you are going to try?"

"I'm not even in Nashville, and I am not sure if I will be back."

"Excuse me. What did you say?" I looked in the back seat of the
car and made sure Cassidy was still asleep.

"Man, I don't know if I will be back in town. The kids are at the
house with my mom. You can drop Cassidy off if you want."

"No, I don't want to drop Cassidy off. Her grades are good, and I
promised her that you were going to hang out with her for her birthday. I don't know what you are doing, but you need to bring your
black ass back to Nashville on Saturday."

"Imma do my best."

"Naw, you gone do better than your best and show the fuck up."

I hung up the phone and shuffled my iPod playlist. I listened to
about six songs and finally my passengers started to wake up.

"Mommy, are we in Paducah, yet?"

"Oh, Cassidy is a real rider, she knows the small town names and
everything," said Darian.

"We are about twenty miles from Paducah, sleepy head."

"Can we get something to eat?" Kalynn was model sized thick and
never missed a meal.

"Yes, it will have to be quick. We don't want to miss the pep
rally." I shuffled my playlist and skipped through a few songs until I
found a song that everyone in the car recognized. We played Biggie
and 112, SWV, Total and I almost skipped over YoYo until Cassidy
spoke up.

"Wait momma, you passed up my song."

"What's your song?

"You Caint Play with my YoYo."

"Lil Girl, what do you know about that? I played the song and little
Miss Cassidy went into full YoYo mode.

Cassidy edited the few curse words in her sing-a-long version, and I couldn't believe my baby knew all of the words. I joined in and the twins cracked up.

"Have you talked to my daddy?"

"Yes, I called him while you were asleep."

"Is he going to pick me and Niyah up from Ms. Kim's house tomorrow?"

"Yes, but he did not give me a time yet." I lie. I lied. I lied. I was angry at the fact that I felt the need to lie. Cassidy was staying 30 minutes away from her father tomorrow, and this should be a no brainer situation.

"Good." She said with relief. After a few more sing-a-longs and conversations with the twins about what they should expect from their college experience we arrived at Gentry Hall and joined the magic in progress.

Cassidy remembered the scene from her childhood. She was literally raised on campus. The twins were in a state of shock and awe. My brothers and sisters grew up in a predominantly white suburb of St. Louis, and they never saw this many black people at one time in their lives. The band played and emitted a voltage that made the majorettes move fiercely. The crowd swayed back and forth and side to side. Members of the Divine Nine stepped and paraded in the center of the stage as if every drum and every brass instrument were solely dedicated to their founders. I joined in the Line of Fortitude and watched my daughter and siblings star gaze at me and my sorority sisters.

After the pep-rally, Cassidy went with Kim and the twins and I headed to the suburbs to stay with my good friend, Casee. We drove and drove through a suburb of Nashville that I did not think existed. We passed a cow pasture before finally arriving at her home. Casee was a stay-at-home mother of three children, and she was facing one of the lowest times of her life, but she held it all together with grace. I was aware of the details of her current tribulation, but this weekend was not about a trial or a tribulation. It was about homecoming. We came in the door partying.

"Get geeked. Get geeked. It's homecoming week. We don't go to work, and we don't go to sleep. We stay up 24/7 the whole week long. I said get geeked." We chanted through the door and her kids came rushing down the steps.

"Darian, this is my good friend, Casee."

"Hello." He replied maturely and shook her hand.

"Casee, this is my sister, Kalynn." They nodded and soon the twins began to talk to Casee as if they were old friends.

On Friday night we socialized, ate pizza, and relaxed. I was so tired from being on the road all day and really needed time to catch up on some rest and relaxation. I called Chris about two dozen times to confirm plans for Cassidy the following day to no avail. If Casee could enjoy our company with all that she was currently going through, I was definitely not going to spoil the weekend by focusing on Chris and his mess of a life. Saturday came and still no word from Chris. I called Kim.

"Kim, I'm not sure if Chris is going to make it. Is Cassidy having a good time?"

"Yes, they are destroying the house, but they are having a good time. Cassidy is so sweet. I love it when she comes to visit."

"Cassidy is going to be so disappointed once she finds out that Chris is not going to pick them up."

"Based on our last conversation, I figured that he might flake out, so I told the girls that I would take them to the movies later. She didn't mention her dad, so she might be ok."

"I hope so, thanks girl. I will call you later." I painted on a happy face with my MAC cosmetics. I'm not sure what Casee used to paint on her happy face but it had to be equally as good because we were both beaming and ready for the night.

The tailgating experience was everything the twins thought it would be and more. The smell of barbecue perfumed the air and red solo cups were a part of the uniform. DJs played the latest music, and there were dozens of outdoor parties going on all at once. We danced and Casee and I drank enough to earn the right to just walk around and sober up. I called Chris. Still no answer, and then I called

Kim to inform her to move forward with her original plans. I joined the party scene as if pain and drama did not spill on the front of my shirt and moved the baby daddy drama to the imma deal with that motherfucka later portion of my brain.

The following morning Casee prepared a full southern breakfast. A spread of smothered potatoes with caramelized onions, grits and biscuits served with peach preserves and maple bacon waited patiently for us.

"Good Morning, did you sleep well?" Casee was aware of my dilemma with Chris, just as I was aware of her dilemma, but as we blessed our food and thanked God for the hands that prepared it, I silently requested that the food have an amnesia effect on my mind in addition to nourishment for my body.

"Morning, I slept like a baby. I'm glad that I am not hung over. My red cup stayed full during my tailgating tour yesterday. The more that I drank the more people poured into my cup. I lost count of my refills."

"I didn't go in as hard as you. I knew that I was driving. Plus, I knew that I wanted to make breakfast for ya'll before you hit the road." Casee grabbed plates from the cabinet and pulled out forks and knives.

"You did not have to make breakfast. We could have grabbed something quick on the road."

"I'm glad she did." Darian added to the conversation and went straight for the bacon. Kalynn also made her morning debut, and we all started tearing into the breakfast. I stared at the jar of peach preserves mentally plotting on my next move. Chris is going to pay for this one. I am not leaving Nashville without him getting a piece of my mind.

"Jazzmine, are you ok? You zoned out on us." Darian noticed my distance, and he could tell that my mind was preoccupied with a heavy thought.

"Casee do you have any poster board?"

"I doubt it. I only buy things like that when the kids have a school project." She looked around the room for a replacement to my request and walked into her office. She never asked why I needed a poster board.

"I know! Give me the cardboard pizza boxes from yesterday and some duct tape."

"O....K...." Her eyes were wide and her motions were slow.

"Do you have a Sharpie or a magic marker?"

"Yep."

"How about tampons?"

"No, I'm out of tampons. I have few panty liners." At this point, my audience knew that I had lost my mind, and I was at the cusp of flipping out.

"Don't worry about the tampons. Chris lives right next to a pharmacy. I will pick some up before I go to his house." I said.

"Are we picking up Cassidy from Chris's house before we leave? I thought she was still at Miss Kim's house?" Kalynn asked.

"Cassidy is still at Kim's. We are going to make a stop at Chris's house before we pick her up. I have a note that I want to leave on Chris's door."

I taped the two pizza boxes together, and in big letters I wrote the most emasculating message ever written. My audience read my poster and no one asked any questions. I didn't have to explain what was bothering me at the moment, and I carried on as if I had signed a hallmark card.

"Is everybody packed and ready to roll?" I pulled my bags into the living room.

"I will take the bags to the car." My brothers were all such gentleman. My father taught them so well. Chris had a great father as well. I can't explain what the hell happened to him.

"Thanks, girl for the hospitality, and do you mind if I keep your duct tape? " I looked like I was up to something. "I am sorry the weekend had to end like this."

"I understand. Shit happens. Believe me I know." We hugged and went our separate ways. We left, without much fuss about the situation.

I didn't leave in tears, and as we departed, she wore the same smile on her face that she wore when we arrived.

We made the stop to the pharmacy. I purchased a cheap box of tampons and pushed them out of the applicators. I used the entire box as ornaments for my poster. When I arrived at Chris's home, I didn't knock on the door. I politely taped the giant size handmade card on his door and smoothly drove away.

I hated the fact that my siblings had to see this moment. We talked a little about the situation, and I talked even more about the importance of waiting to engage in serious relationships. I was only a few years older than them when I made the decision to settle down with Chris. I loved him, and I naïvely felt that we would grow together. I believed that having love for a person was enough to build a life together. I thought that most men were secure and chivalrous like my dad and brothers and because of this trust poured from my heart freely. Life has proved to me quite the opposite, and my clean heart has been the blank canvas for the insecure men that I have decided to invite into my life. They have sketched their insecurities onto me and when my eraser runs thin, I go off.

I was certain that I had not over reacted to Chris's absence. The note was poignant full of passion, and my intentions were from the deepest sutures of my heart.   My role as a mother requires daily prayer, planning, and sacrifices. Chris's only role consists of a few cameos a year. I should be able to depend on him to do that. On the way home I never mentioned Chris and once again I had to come up with a lie to cover for him. I am sick of covering for him; I had to wrap birthday gifts and Christmas gifts that Ryan paid for and we put Chris's name on the gift tags. I hope he was offended by my poster, and I hope it prepares him for Hell. Yes, Hell because God is a single black women with a child. And any man who does not take care of his kids is not getting into the pearly gates of Heaven. He's going to hell.

The Greatest Performance of My Life

I TOLD RYAN everything that happened over the weekend. He was always so good about lifting my spirits when I was at my lowest. When I arrived home, he met me at my condo with dinner. Later that week, he took Cassidy to dinner for her birthday and took her on a mini shopping spree. He's not the husband of my dreams, but he is a good spousal equivalent at times.

I always made November responsible for a smooth Christmas in December. I made out my grocery and gift lists and checked in with my friends and co-workers to make sure that I was on target. I scheduled a meeting with my work counterpart, Ty. We both wanted to make sure we closed the sales year strong.

We chose a small tea room in our work territory, called Josephine's. Technically, it wasn't his choice. It was my choice, but he agreed. The dining area was an oversized living room that could seat around a hundred people comfortably. The lavish early American décor made me feel like we were visiting a rich Midwestern aunt. Women traveled in tour busses to taste the sinful homemade desserts. I personally loved dipping the homemade rolls into the warm lobster bisque.

"It's another man in sight. I think I am losing a little bit of my manhood by eating with you at this place."

During our conversation, I shared an edited version of my homecoming experience. I didn't' breathe one word about the banner that I plastered on my child's father's door. The first part of the conversation was strictly personal. I asked him about what he planned to buy his kids for Christmas, and he ran a few ideas by me in regards to the perfect surprise for his beautiful, sweet hearted new wife. He planned to buy her a few gifts. One of them was an iPod preloaded with all of the songs that reminded him of his love for her. I remember when they first started dating. He would talk about her and how they met in college. It was the cutest thing ever to see my very serious partner transform into a 16-year-old boy whenever he talked about his wife, Stacee. A successful black man giddy about love, daydreaming of ways to make his queen's life special, gives me hope.

At the end of our conversation Ty, informed me that he was resigning from the company, and he was going to explore an opportunity that would almost double his salary. I was so excited for him and nervous at the same time. A new team mate could mean a career disaster. The pharmaceutical industry was full of two-faced sociopaths, and I had been fortunate enough to never have to work with any of them. I used the long Thanksgiving weekend to celebrate the holiday and my birthday.

I hosted a black Friday brunch. The event did not have a starting time nor an ending time. Friends and family would stop by and eat and drink in between shopping mall runs. My flagship recipes for my brunch were always the French toast casserole and an oven baked omelet. Also on the menu was an assortment of hors d'oeuvres, fruit salad, and beef tenderloin. Each dish sat in fancy serving ware and my table was staged appropriately for a Southern Living photo shoot.

On black Friday, Erin and I chose to meet up at Target. Neither one of us came with a shopping agenda. We just enjoyed spectating. Together we spent about $20 and just after 10 in the morning we made it to my condo. All of the food was ready. I only had to put the French toast casserole in the oven for about 45 minutes. I pulled out a pitcher filled with pomegranate mimosas. My speaker blasted my playlist of throwback Christmas songs from, Marvin Gaye, Smokey Robinson, The Jackson Five, and the Temptations and new school classics from Chris Brown, Mariah Carey, and Destiny's Child. It was beginning to sound and smell like Christmas.

"I'm not used to your house being this quiet."

"Me either." Cassidy went to visit her dad for the Thanksgiving holiday. Her grandparents on her father's side of the family lived close by, and they were headed to Nashville to visit Chris and other family members in Tennessee. They were award winning grandparents, and they always rounded up their grandkids for road trips. My poster may have inspired the trip.

"I couldn't believe you let Cody go to Kansas City with his dad."

"Ryan invited me to go with him to Kansas City. He had business to take care in some small town just outside of Kansas City on Tuesday. Ryan's best friend and his wife were hosting a huge Thanksgiving dinner and Ryan really wanted to stay in Kansas City for the holiday. Thanksgiving is my grandmother's favorite holiday of the year, and she has been really ill, so I didn't want to trade in dinner in Kansas City for dinner at my Granny's. He will be back later today."

"I get all of that, but Ryan could have rolled his happy ass to Kansas City and Cody could have stayed with you." Her eyes rolled as she slowly sipped her mimosa.

"Since Cassidy, spent Thanksgiving with her dad, Ryan felt that Cody should spend Thanksgiving with him. We had a huge blow up about how I monopolized all of the holidays. I let him win so I did not have to have this conversation during Christmas." I slammed a half full mimosa down my throat and walked to the Kitchen for my third round.

"You want another glass, Erin?"

"No, I'm nursing, and I already have to pump and dump. I don't want to overdo it."

Erin's beautiful baby boy was about two months old. I had to get used to her being a mother. I'd became accustomed to her footloose and fancy free lifestyle, but Erin was a natural mother.

I put on my favorite movie of all times, Eddie Murphy's *Coming to America* and laughed at the movie as if I did not know every line. Right after Sexual Chocolate dropped the Mike, I heard a knock on the door. It was my brother Keith and his wife, Tecia with my niece Kiera and nephew Keith III. I opened the door and they both yelled happy birthday in unison.

"Here Jazz, this is for you." Tecia handed me two wrapped gifts. I loved surprises, and I didn't expect them to buy me a gift.

"It's just a little somethin, somethin." My brother said. My enthusiasm made him a little nervous, and he wanted to blunt my expectations. Only a small fraction of my reaction was due to the gifts, the vodka in the pomegranate mimosa was responsible for the greater portion.

"Whatever it is, I appreciate it. Go ahead and make a plate. I gave my niece and nephew juicy drunk auntie kisses.

"Where are Cassidy and Cody?" My 6-year-old nephew was very observant, and he knew that there was an unusual calmness in my house. I was just glad that my nephew was not in the hospital during the holidays. He had a rare disorder, and he spent his life in and out of the hospital.

"They are both out of town. You guys can watch television in my room."

"Ok, T-T Jazz, that's fine with me. Come on Kiera."

"Ya'll want something to drink?" The more I drank, the more southern I became.

"What do you think? Now, Jazz that was a silly question. This food is the bomb dot come, and all I need is something to wash it down with."

It was around 2ish when my mother knocked on the door.

"Happy Birthday, on this day, 31 years ago, I became the mother of a beautiful baby girl and I am so proud of the woman she has become 31 years later." My mom overdosed on Less Brown and Iyanla Vanzant in the early 90's, and she could sound like a moving Hallmark card or a live fortune cookie whenever she got into her zone.

Plates and forks were clicking and clacking. The pomegranate mimosa had taken its effect on my brother, Tecia and my mom. Poor Erin passed out on the couch after she fed Chase the last of the pre-pumped milk.

"Let me tell you what happened at my school this week." My mom opened all of her classroom tales this way. "Now there is this little boy in kindergarten that Miss Jackson has to send to the office every other day for cursing. I pulled the little boy over to the side during recess for cursing and told him he had to spend five minutes in time out. He said, "Shit Miss Jones, my bad!" At that point, I knew he had a serious problem. Then during a fire drill, he ran down the hall screaming, "Run for your fucking lives, this motherfucka bouta burn." Miss Jackson had him suspended, and he couldn't come back to school until she conferenced with one of his parents. When the mother showed up she said, "I told him about that bullshit. He was doing the same mothafuckin shit at daycare."

We laughed to keep from crying.

"Hey good people, we are about to head out of here. Let's cut the cake." The cake was beautiful and it read, Happy Birthday Bestie, Love Erin." Everyone sang happy birthday and said their goodbyes.

For the first time all day, my house was quiet and empty. I washed the dishes and put the leftover food in Tupperware containers. I placed the cake in the center of the table and used it as a makeshift centerpiece.

As I looked at the cake and my watch, I realized that it was 5 o'clock and Ryan had not picked up the phone to call me and wish me a happy birthday. And I hadn't picked up the phone to wish my Aunt Lynn a happy birthday either. My Aunt Lynn was my father's youngest sister, and we were born on the same day.

"Happy birthday, Auntie."

"Thank you, I heard you were having a brunch today. How did it turn out?"

"The food was good, and I made a drink from a recipe, that I found online called a pomegranate mimosa. I drank half of the pitcher, and I am two shades in the wind right now." I heard my aunt laugh her infamous, high pitched, vibrating laugh.

"You should have come in town Auntie. Thanksgiving dinner was great. There was enough food to go around, and nobody fought and nobody had to call the police. What did you do for your birthday?" I asked in one long breath.

"Not much. We went to the movies and I just chilled around the house. What did Ryan get you for your birthday?"

My aunt knew that Ryan's gifts were more like gag gifts than birthday surprises, and she never missed the opportunity to expose him as a waist of my time.

"I'm not sure yet. He went to Kansas City. I guess I will see when he gets back." I didn't tell her that he hadn't even called to wish me a happy birthday. I didn't want to get all worked up, and he still had a few hours before it was an official snooze on my birthday.

Chris missed child support payments, but he was always one of the first people to wish me a happy birthday. Ryan didn't even do that. Before the conversation went even deeper into the actions of Ryan, I was saved by the bell. I noticed out of the window that my father was pulling up with the car fully loaded with Lisa, the twins, and my younger brother Tyler.

"Auntie, let me call you back. Your brother just pulled up. Leave it up to them to show up after I have cleaned up the kitchen."

"You know how my brother is. Call me later, love you."

"I love you too." I didn't care that they were late, and all of the food was packed up. I was just glad they were here so that I could reset my mind back to happy instead of focusing on Ryan.

"Hey Daddy." I gave him the same hug and kiss that I remembered giving my dad when I was a little girl, and I passed hugs and kisses around the room.

"You said that you were having brunch and by the looks of things. The party ended at 3 o'clock on the nose."

"I told ya'll, I was having a brunch. It's after 5. What did you expect?"

"You know how we do. Our celebrations are built to last."

"We can keep the party going. I will mix up a batch of pomegranate mimosas at 5 pm."

"Yes bring on the mi...mo...sas." Lisa chimed in.

I retold my mom's story about the kindergartener with the cursing problem. We philosophized on the challenges of our school systems. My dad blamed every inner city circumstance on rap music. My siblings and I made a salient effort to defend rap, but we lost. We hugged, and they made their way back to the suburbs.

I went straight to my room and spent around an hour thanking God for my family and allowing me to see my 31st birthday. I thanked him for the health of my family, and I asked for forgiveness for being upset because Ryan did not make it to my brunch or call me on my birthday. I stared at my cell phone from 11:58 until 12:00 am the next day. He never called. I felt tears brewing, but there were none left. I have cried buckets of tears over this man. I didn't cry. I wept. I could feel my chest sinking in and my nose took in extra breaths of air until I fell asleep.

The sun peaked through my window, and I reached for the remote and turned on the news. Maybe Ryan was in a bad car accident, and he was lying in a hospital bed somewhere between Kansas City and St. Louis. I watched the news waiting to hear a report about a 10-car pile-up. It never came, and the weather girl reported that St. Louis would have a record high of 70 degrees. In late November I thought, but that was true St. Louis weather for you. Before I jumped to a conclusion that would ruin this beautiful November day, I chose to worry about Ryan's safety.

I called his cell phone. I heard it ring, but no one answered. I left a message and waited. Then I sent a text message. A neutral message that read: JUST CHECKING ON YOU GIVE ME A CALL. This was the first of five messages that I sent, and I spent the next three hours calling his cell phone. I am ashamed to say that I dialed his number about 30 times, before I finally called his mother.

"Mrs. Sanders, how are you?"

"Fine and you?"

"I'm well. It's a beautiful day, and I can't seem to pull myself together and enjoy it. The holidays are always so busy for me, and I am exhausted."

"I know what you mean. I had to work, and today I am on call at the hospital. I hope they don't call me in to work before I pick up Ryan from the airport."

"What time does his flight get in?" I asked casually.

"At 7:30." She answered without suspicion.

"My Granny surely missed you for dinner. You know she loves talking to you."

"I hate I missed dinner too, but I would have had to get someone to cover for me."

"You heard from Ryan? I called him a few times, and his phone went straight to his voice mail."

"Yeah, I talked to him about an hour ago to make sure I didn't get the flight time mixed up."

"I'm glad you talked to him. I was getting a little worried. People get crazy around the holidays." I said this as I washed my face, with my free hand and looked into the mirror. "Try and enjoy this weather, Mrs. Sanders, and have a good day."

"Alright, you do the same." She hung up the phone oblivious to the fact that our conversation would be used to spark the combustible fumes that had been circulating in my head for the past 33 hours.

I went downstairs and stared at my cake. "He did not call me on my birthday." I said to myself. I threw my own party. My best friend brought the cake and this man did not even call. I sat in the dining chair and gazed at the table. I share the best of me with him. I carried his son for nine months and delivered the boy of his dreams, and he is my worst nightmare. But I'm up now, oh yeah. My ass is up. And at my moment of awakening my pomegranate mimosa saturated brain came up with a plan. "Imma drive an hour away and share my birthday cake with Ryan." I called up Erin to invite her to the party.

"Erin." I didn't say anything else and my voice squeaked as I called her name."

"Jazz, is everything OK?" I pulled myself together and surprisingly my next lines were delivered clearly and devoid of emotions. At times when I speak my tongue allows the ending sounds of my words to float away but my teeth grabbed every sound.

"No, no, not at all. Ryan did not even call me on my birthday, and it's after 12 o'clock, and he still has not called. I will not turn the other cheek, and I am not going to be the bigger person. I don't feel at all rational or reasonable, and I am about to fuck his shit up. I am on my way to his home, and I wanted to know if you would ride out to his house with me?"

"Now, Jazz I know you are upset, and you should be but." I interrupted her sentence.

"Erin, my mind is made up. It is pointless to try and talk sense into my head at this point. The only decision that is flexible is you. I am riding with or without you."

"Alright come and get me. I need to make sure this doesn't get too crazy."

I picked up Erin and most of the ride was in silence. Usually I was a slow patient driver, but today I zoomed down the highway. I was in a zone. Until I heard thump, thump, thump.

"Damn, I have a flat tire." I responded casually as if I had flat tires every other day.

"See, this is a sign from God, Jazz." I called my roadside service, and we waited for about an hour on the side of the highway. On this day, Erin was the perfect disciple of Christ and used as many scriptures as she could think of to illustrate how God saves us from ourselves. Roadside assistance came to the rescue, and I thanked God for blessing me with roadside assistance and proceeded to head in the direction of Ryan's house.

"Are we getting off at the next exit to turn around?"

"No, we are going to Ryan's house donut tire and all. We are going to drive slower, that's all." I arrived at Ryan's home. Went to the front door and attempted to open it. He never locked his doors, but today they were locked. I went to the back of his home and he had a raised wooden deck that did not have stairs leading to the yard. I climbed up the deck throwing my body over the sides of the deck and landing safely near a BBQ pit and a few lounge chairs. I prayed that his patio door was open. This was my last hope. I'm not sure who answered my prayer, but the door was unlocked, and I was in. The house was so quiet, and the walls were watching me. I went upstairs and looked in every trash can. I don't even know why, but I did. I saw a few receipts on his dresser, and I read them. One receipt had a phone number on it, and I put it in my pocket. I guess that was exhibit A or something. I was in another world, and then I heard Erin's voice.

"Get your ass out of this man's house." She screamed.

"OK, OK, I'm ready." I really wanted to empty a bag of flour onto his kitchen floor, but I missed my window of opportunity to do that. I walked out of his home and pulled the cake from the back seat of my car. I removed the cover from the cake and shot putted the cake onto his garage door and smeared it from one side of the door to the other.

As we left we saw several of his neighbors take inventory of the display. One neighbor was biking through the neighborhood, and I saw her reach for her cell phone. That was the biggest crime that was committed in his community all year so I was sure that the police would soon be there.

"Do you feel better bestie?"

"Yes, I do, and I appreciate you for riding with me."

I never cried, and when I returned home, I was absolutely positive that I made the right choice. Even though it was an unorthodox reaction to a circumstance in which someone forgets your birthday, I was justified in doing so. I also convinced myself that I was not bat shit crazy for doing this.

Everybody Loves the Sunshine

I HAD ONE conversation with Ryan about the event, and I denied being anywhere near his home during the time.

"You need to start living right Ryan. Maybe it was one of your closet hoes." I said.

"My neighbors described you to a tee." He replied.

"Did you see me do it?" I asked.

"No."

"Well, it wasn't me." Our conversation ended with us agreeing to end our relationship and work together to raise our son. He never fully explained why he took a flight to Kansas City. He told me that he had to check on a job site near Kansas City. His story never added up, and it never would. Luckily for me my cousin Dee organized a December family cruise, and I spent the next few weekends helping my mother and grandmother prepare for our trip.

My mother was a modern woman. Her home décor was reflective of her personality. It was small by Midwestern standards, but the layout of her home made it appear larger. The furniture was warm, elegant, and simple, a far contrast to her wardrobe.

"Jazzmine, come to my bedroom, I want you to see the clothes that I bought for the trip. I know that you say that I get too carried away with matching up prints, but let me show you what I found at the mall." My eyes widened and I asked for a glass of wine to sip during her trunk show. This is going to be good.

She started with a few outfits, and I gave her credit for the simplicity of her first selections. My mother always dressed age appropriate, and her clothes would fit her nicely, but she had a tendency to overdo it with the prints, colors, and rhinestones. The show had just begun and I was surprised that all of her selections were without bling.

"I am impressed mom. You did a good job."

"Wait. I need your opinion on this one top. I wasn't sure about what I would wear with it, but I loved it, and it was on sale for $9.99." My mother was excited, and she unveiled a peach, tan, and powder blue floral top. My face did little to disguise my contempt for the shirt. It was the absolute worst.

"I can tell by the look on your face that you do not like the top, but look at these pants with it." She held out a peach pair of pencil slacks.

"No, mom. I hate that shirt, and I wish it would die."

"Jazzmine, when I saw this shirt at the store, I noticed the pretty colors, and the shirt just jumped out at me."

"Well, you should have ran." We busted out laughing.

"Imma take it back, but the other stuff I picked was cool right?"

"Yes, overall you did well, mom."

• • •

On the day of the cruise, everyone was hyped up and ready to go. My mother cried. My mom never missed out on a sentimental moment. "I am so happy my family is all here. I remember a time in which the only time we traveled together was to visit my dad and my uncles in jail, and now-a-days we are driving as a family to go to college graduations and vacations." She said this in the airport with an audience of about 15 of my relatives and they felt it, especially my elders.

I enjoyed every second of the cruise and whenever I felt that I was slipping into as zone of sadness. I looked at my brother's smile and watched my sister-n-law dance. I had conversations with relatives that I only saw during holidays, and I felt even closer to my close knit family and my grandmother was having more fun than all of us. My mother and I went to a game show and my grandmother stayed behind. When we returned back to the room, I could not believe my eyes.

"Nanny, what are you doing?" My grandmother had a bottle of red nail polish and was polishing the last unpainted toenail.

"What does it look like? I am polishing my toes."

"When was the last time you polished your toes?"

"It has probably been over 20 years ago."

"I'm tellin my granddaddy on you." I said in my 10-year-old little girl voice.

"What happens on the cruise stays on the cruise." One would have thought that the red nail polish would be the return of Kool Aide and the end of Mother Miller, the way my grandmother said that. I guess my grandmother called herself getting ready for the beach in Nassau. Oddly, she didn't wear open toe shoes or sandals. The next day we would spend the entire day in Nassau. I was looking forward to the day at the beach. I had a playlist ready specifically for the beach, and I had a book and some gossip magazines packed and ready to go.

The beach was everything that we as a family needed it to be. The air was warm and crisp. The waves floated in and out and created the perfect lullaby for a lounge chair nap. I spotted a nearby cabana where a massage therapist was giving beachside massages.

"Hey guys, I will be right back. I am going to check the prices for the massages." The massage was only $30 for 30 minutes. I went back to get money from my beach tote.

"How much was it?" My mom asked without true interest.

"It's only $30, and you have to pay in cash."

"Oh well, I guess I won't be getting one. I only brought $10 cash with me. The rest of my money is on the ship." My mother returned to her book, and I headed towards the cabana.

The male masseuse had a deep brown complexion, and he was in his mid 40's. His appearance was neither repulsive nor attractive. It had been almost a month since I felt the touch of a man, and it made me notice his swag.

I had on a bathing suit with a pair of short blue jean shorts. I removed the shorts and laid on the massage table. He covered my body with a white sheet and pulled the sheet back to expose my back. The sound of the waves passing in and out set the mood. He began to work his hands through the tension on my neck and shoulders. He moved from my neck to my back and kneaded the lower part of my back. He then covered my back with the sheet and uncovered my left leg. He worked his hands through my inner and outer thigh, down to my calve muscle, and then to my foot and did the very same thing for my right leg. With every touch, my body felt lighter and lighter. After the massage was over, I put on my shorts and wanted to say, "Call me."

I didn't walk back to the lounge chair area, I floated. My nostrils were flared and my small slanted eyes were even tighter. I was embarrassed for my mom and grandmother to see this expression on my face, but I couldn't control it.

"How much did you say that massage cost?" My mom asked intensely.

"Thirty dollars."

"Do you have any cash on you?"

"No."

"Mom do you have any cash?" My mom scrambled for massage money, and I relaxed in the lounge chairs and pulled out a magazine.

"Excuse me your majesty." I heard a thick Bahamian accent. I looked up and saw a man that I noticed earlier recruiting people for jet ski tours. *He must be really desperate for jet ski tourist if he is referring to me as your majesty.*

"Yes." I answered as if I was always referred to as your majesty.

"Have you ever road on a jet ski before?"

"No."

"Would you like to ride the jet ski?"

"I would like to, but I don't have any cash left."

"Your ride is on the house." Jet ski tours cost at least $60 and my free offer made Nanny suspicious.

"Why you gone let her ride for free?" Nanny did not trust anything free.

"She's beautiful."

"Here, look at my badge; I work for the tour company." I looked at his badge and it looked official enough.

"I'm going." At 31 years old, I didn't need permission to leave. My family only needed to know where I was going.

"Uh hum, what's your name again sir? We gone write it down on a piece of paper. I didn't pack my pistol with me, but I can find a knife somewhere on this island." I was not surprised at my grandmother's threat. She had several stories from her past laced with pistols. I even saw my grandmother shoot a gun at somebody when I was little kid. She was not playing.

I sashayed my tail towards the jet ski and the adventure began. I grabbed his waist and we cut through the deep waves of the sea. The tides were unusually high and each dip felt like a mini roller coaster drop. I held on tighter to his waist. Then it dawned on me, "My life is in this man's hands." I was no longer independent. I needed this strange Bahamian man's ability to navigate to survive. It was the closest that I had come to truly needing a man outside of my father in my life. It was a great feeling.

My free tour included a port stop to a seaside bar. I ordered a Bahama mamma and sipped it at the bar.

"What did you say your name was, beautiful?"

"You can just continue to call me Beautiful."

"That's fine. Are you married beautiful?"

"No."

"How is that? A man has not asked you to marry him as beautiful as you are? Don't you want children someday?" He was killing my Bahama mamma buzz, and I knew that this survey was not a part of the tour.

"I already have children." I replied. He told me that he also had children and we discussed their ages and made small talk about our kids.

"Do you smoke?" He asked.

"No."

"Do you mind if I smoke?"

"Will you be able to drive me back safely?"

"Certainly."

"Smoke away."

He smoked on the dock of the sea side bar, and I sipped what was left of the strongest Bahama mamma that I ever had in my life. I placed my feet on the rocks in the water, and I was close enough to the smoke to get a contact high. The sun, the sips, and the smoke yielded a mental orgasm.

This experience coupled with my massage from earlier showed up in my expressions and the tour guide asked me if I had plans for later. I didn't want to reject him harshly. I did need him to take me back to the other side of the island. So I invited him to a club that someone suggested on the cruise ship that I had no interest in going to.

"We've been gone for a long time. We better get back so that my family does not start to worry."

We headed back and with every dip, I made a squeaky noise that was fun to me but erotic to my tour guide. As we approached the shore I noticed that all of the lounge chairs had been stashed away and the beach looked more like a deserted island. I saw my grandmother's hands reaching to the sky as we neared the beach I began to hear what she was shouting.

"Thank you! Thank you Jesus! Jesus! Jesus! Jesus, thank you heavenly Father." I was so fixated with my grandmother's beachside worship service that I did not notice my mother behind me with a shoe.

"Where in the fuck have you been?" She slammed the shoe on the side of my ass as hard as she could.

"Momma." She hit me with a flip flop at the rate of about 80 licks per minute as I hopped through the sand. My sister-in-law's, eyes were pink from crying, and she and my brother were relieved that I was getting my ass whooped. My mother ran out of breath and dropped the shoe which was ironically mine.

"Go find your other damn shoe so that we can get back to the ship." The beach was shut down early due to the high tides of the sea. For the past 35 minutes my family wondered why a jet ski tour that cost $60 only lasted for 15 minutes and my tour that was free lasted for an hour and a half. Together, they concluded that my tour was free because the tour guide had kidnapped me. Natalie Holloway was fresh on their minds and in 45 minutes they had already planned my funeral and visualized living life without me.

By dinner time all of my closest family and friends were aware of my beachside whoopin. It was bad enough that my mom beat me with my own shoe, but she didn't have to tell the entire family. The story made my cousin Charlotte furious. I looked over, and I saw death and destruction in Charlotte's eyes. She was rubbing her jeans and rocking back and forth.

"I wish you was my daughter, I would have Fucked...You...Up."

This was not a joke. I moved to the other side of the room. If Charlotte snapped, I wanted to have a running start. No one in the room said that I should not have received a beating on my vacation. Clearly no one cared that I was an adult with a job, a mortgage, and kids. In their minds, mother was just, and I did not argue with anyone. I just listened. All of my maternal relatives look like they whoop ass for fun, and I could be jumped for pissing off my mother. All she had to do was give them a nod. The ship did not leave for the next port of call until 5 a.m. I wondered if I would be allowed to leave the ship and explore the nightlife of the Bahamas.

"Dee, can I get you a drink? Charmane, would you like some more ice tea?" I had the complete posture of a 7-year-old after a good spanking, and I wanted to make sure I was in my cousin's good graces. I stayed clear of Charlotte, but I was extra polite to everyone else. When the time came to get dressed to go out to the club, I pulled out my clothes and started to get dressed as if nothing happened.

"Now you stay with the group, Jazzmine. Don't leave period. If you go to the bathroom make sure someone goes with you."

"Yeah and if you walk away from your drink, leave it there, and don't drink it." Nanny added. I had my 16th birthday 15 years ago, but by their advice you would think that I was celebrating it on this cruise.

"I know. I know." I wished I could have had a second take at my response. I would remove the sarcasm and slight eye roll that I had dished out, but this was live.

"I don't know what the hell your ass knows because your stupid ass could have been kidnapped earlier today." Hell was in my mom's eyes, and she wanted to beat me again.

"Momma it was the…." I'll quit while I'm ahead. "Yes Ma'am." Her advice was coming from a place of love, so there was no need to battle it.

The night was young. I was rolling with my sister-in-law and a few of my younger cousins. My brother was sick and did not make it off of the cruise ship. The ultimate party package for me included drinking a few alcoholic beverages, dancing until my feet were sore, and flirting with whomever I determined was the hottest man in the

room. I was not into sex with strange men, drugs, or anything else
that I could not discuss with my ironically conservative social circle.

"Would you like to dance?" An average looking Bahamian man
asked. His accent and manners made him more attractive to me, and
I said yes. We danced for two consecutive songs.

"Would you like me to buy you a drink?"

"Yes."

"I will be right back."

"No, I will come with you." I knew that taking a drink from a
stranger was a no no, and the drink had to be put directly into my
hands from the bartender. I ordered a Bahama mamma and the average looking man started a competition with my shadow. Wherever I
went, he followed and every song was his jam. After the sixth song,
I realized that the drink that he purchased for me was not a kind gesture. It was an investment, and I could not get rid of him. I ran over
to my kicking it crew.

"Excuse me I will be right back." I told my shadow.

"Where are you going?" Seriously, he wanted a reason.

"To the restroom." I am glad that my relatives were not here to
witness this conversation. They would have called me a punk ass in
front of my shadow's face. I rounded up my posse, and we all went
to the restroom.

"This man will not leave me alone. What should I do?"

"Tell him to go dance with someone else."

"If that does not work tell him to get the hell out of your face."
Dionne added.

I left the bathroom feeling empowered. After I saw a handsome,
well-dressed man sitting near the DJ booth, I came up with a bright
idea. My shadow floated towards me as soon as I left the bathroom.
I think he was watching the bathroom door.

"Are you ready to dance?"

"No, I had a great time with you, but the person that I came to
meet here just arrived."

"Who are you here to meet?" I pointed to my target. "Dano, you are here to meet Dano?"

"Yes." I was so glad that he dropped his name.

"Where did you meet Dano?"

"I met him earlier today at the beach."

"You are a liar." My shadow became crazy and angry, and if I had my Eckhart Tolle audiobook with me, I would have given it to him.

"That's rude, and I am offended. I met him at the beach."

"I have known Dano my entire life, and he never goes to the beach."

"Well, he did today." I quickly walked towards Dano, and I thanked God that I was able to escape my crazy shadow. I had faith that I was being delivered into a better situation.

I didn't ask him his name right away, I just started to dance. My crew was having a good time. I scanned the crowd and Dano was by far the most handsome man in the room, and he immediately became my flirt target for the evening.

The DJ switched from reggae to American music and Trey Songs *Say Ahh* blasted through the speakers. I started dancing on Dano's lap. My crew noticed me and they found targets for themselves. Everyone was sweating and having a good time. We danced through the next four songs.

"Thank You." I told him.

"Thank you for what?" He was confused as to why the beautiful woman who had just given him a free lap dance thanked him.

"You saved me from that crazy man over there. He wanted to dance with me the entire night."

"Men in the Bahamas are very possessive. You are a beautiful woman, and he didn't want any other man to try and dance with you." He said with a smile.

"What's your name?" I asked as a formality.

"Dano and yours?"

"Jazzmine."

"Jazzmine, that is a beautiful name. How long will you be in the Bahamas?"

"The ship leaves early in the morning."

"Oh you are with a cruise line?"

"Yes." I wanted him to continue to ask him questions so that I could hear him speak.

As the night grew older we danced and talked and we danced and talked some more. He had an American swag about him and I liked him. When it was time to leave, he escorted us back to the ship, and I knew that I would see him again. His accent and smile felt like sunshine.

Just Fine

MY CHILDREN PLAYED between the kitchen and the hallway and the living room. We sat in Erin's small eat in kitchen. Erin offered me a glass of wine, and I politely accepted and sipped while she baked the last of her Christmas desserts. I had already given her all of the details of my Bahamas excursion.

"So, are you going to see him again?" She sipped her wine and gave an ooo la la look.

"Are you asking me if I am going to an island to visit a strange man that I met at the club?"

"Or he can come St. Louis."

"It's not like that. I just like talking to him. His voice is soothing and his conversation is upbeat. I needed something to get Ryan off of my mind, and it's doing the trick."

"Are you hungry? I baked some chicken earlier," Erin rearranged clutter from the kitchen countertop.

"Yes, that sounds good to me."

"I'm so pissed at my little cousin."

"Which one?"

"Desiree."

"What did she do this time?" Desiree was a beautiful little girl that grew up to be a complicated teenage mom.

"She was charged as accessory to armed robbery."

"What?" I said in disbelief. She did not have the ways of a hard street criminal. Desiree was a quiet girl and I could probably rob her with a picture of a gun.

"She was messing around with her stupid baby daddy. That dumb ass man robbed a liquor store while Desiree was in the car. They made out his license plate and arrested him and her. He was charged with armed robbery, and she was charged as an accessory."

"Was she driving the car?"

"No. She wasn't driving but according to the law you don't have to drive the getaway car to get charged"

"She won't do any jail time will she?"

"She is facing a 10-year prison sentence."

"Ten years!"

"Yes, my mom had to retain a lawyer for $10,000. That is money that could be used for my son's college fund. I don't understand how she makes such bad decisions and how she gets into the stupid shit that she does. I have worked hard to be a role model for her. I have tried to help her get into school. My mother and I have tried our damnedest to show her a better way."

"She grew up differently than you did."

"I understand that Jazz, but she has small children to raise. She has to start thinking about her babies."

My kids grew restless and their playing turned into fighting. I toggled between a conversationalist and a referee with ease. Then Toni, Erin's neighbor, walked into the house and joined the fireside chat.

"Jazzmine, you are going to have stop calling my phone and hanging up. If you want something from me all your fine ass has to do is ask?" Toni laughed and his round cheeks vibrated.

"I didn't want to cause any trouble with your women, but I will keep that in mind next time." I played into the joke and caressed his shoulder.

"You still fucking with that nigga?" Unfortunately Toni was at Erin's house on the day that I lost my mind and was aware of my insanity episode.

"No, we are done."

"I don't understand the shit. You are beautiful. You are a good mother, and you have a lot going for yourself. If that nigga don't want to marry you, fuck him. You too fine to be driving down the highway with cakes and shit. Is the dick that good?"

"We are not together Toni. I'm good."

"That's what your mouth say, but your heart is still with that nigga. As soon as he gets sick of the bitch that he is messing with, ya'll gone get back together."

"Have you finished your Christmas shopping?" I changed the subject.

"Yes, I'm done." Toni gave us the run down on the gifts that he had purchased, and the ladies of his life were going to make out very well during the Christmas season.

"See, I don't understand you and Erin. Ya'll have way too much shit to put up with all the shit that ya'll put up with," words spoken from a true front porch philosopher.

In Color

ON MY WAY to work, I received a call from my Dad. We usually spoke a couple of times a week, but my conversations with Dano had replaced our time.

"Hey Beanie, you put your old man down? You only call me when you get bored." Beanie was my toddler name that only my dad used.

"No, Dad. I didn't put you down. I have just been in my own world."

"How's work going?"

"Work is going well as far as my sales numbers are concerned. I am getting a new team mate, and I am a little concerned."

"What's the problem?"

"People are telling me that he's ultra conservative and a border-line racist. This could be a disaster."

"What did they tell you that he was involved in to give him this reputation?"

"They haven't really said."

"Listen. Don't react to someone else's bad experience with another person. You don't know the nature of his previous colleagues. That is not to say that he didn't rightfully earn his reputation, but give him a chance to establish a reputation with you based on who you are as a professional and based on your company culture." My father's advice was very sound, and my anxieties with working with my new teammate were extinguished. I attended church quarterly, but I prayed every night. I prayed on this situation. I asked God to continue to bless my professional relationships.

Colin, my new teammate, and I met for the first time at the unofficial headquarters of all pharmaceutical representatives, Panera. He was tall and attractive in a Friday Night lights sort of way.

"Welcome aboard." I firmly shook his hand and sat across the table.

"Hey now, I've heard a lot about you."

"I didn't do it." I said jokingly and hoped that my report was better than his.

He casually told me why he was excited to join the company. It mostly had to do with the fact that his previous company was always laying off sales professional, and he was impressed with the pipeline of new products in our company. He showed me pictures of his family, and I showed him pictures of my children. He knew that I was a single parent and although our lifestyles were different, we talked with ease about our children.

"So what do you do for fun?"

"I like to travel with my family. I read a lot. Whenever I get a chance, I happy hour hop with my friends. How about you?"

"My family and I vacation in South Carolina every year. We rent a house and a few other families join us. I go to a bar or two when I get a kitchen pass from my wife."

"Is the house on the beach?"

"Yes and the house has a pool. It's very nice. The kids play. We grill, and I try not to overdo my booze."

"Sounds like fun." I kept my responses and questions generic.

"About five years ago, I learned to play the guitar. I play at local bars whenever I'm booked. I have a gig at the winery in Grafton. You should come and bring a date."

"I will come. I'm not sure if my date will make it." I smiled.

"Do you listen to Howard?"

"Howard who?"

"Oh, you have to get out more. You don't know who Howard Stern is?"

"Yes, I've heard of Howard Stern, but I have never really listened to his show."

"It's hilarious. You should start tuning in. It helps the long drives go by faster." I did start to listen to the Howard Stern Show. My teammate was also a devout Rush Limbaugh and Glenn Beck listener as well. I was more familiar with Rush and Glenn than Stern. My parents were big proponents of listening to two sides of every story. I encouraged Collin to listen to Al Sharpton and Joe Madison. I am not sure if he tuned in. I wanted him to be enlightened as well. Collin was a proud Tea Party Republican, and I truly did not see one party as a true winner. *I think that they both might lose.*

I went to his performance at a winery in Grafton on the bank of the Mississippi River. It was early March, and it was not warm enough for the performance to take place outdoors. The space was small and decorated like an upscale juke joint. Collin was on a small stage with a friend of his that played the bass guitar. I could tell by his expression that he didn't expect me to show up. I recognized a few receptionists from the nearby doctor's office and joined them at a table and ordered a beer. They were shocked.

He played Superstitious by Stevie Wonder, and I hit the dance floor. Then it happened. He handed me the cow bell. Everybody knows that you can never have enough cow bell, and I beat it to the rhythm of the beat.

"More Cowbell."

"More Cowbell."

L is for

MY FATHER WAS very close to our relatives in Little Rock, Arkansas. My daddy understood how to squeeze the juice out of life and made it a point to walk down memory lane. My brothers and sisters toured his childhood hometown in North Little Rock. He pointed to old worn down shacks like they had once been mansions belonging to families of distinction. We were headed to a family reunion. I'm not sure how we were related to the family members that we came to visit. The relatives were not on our family tree, but they did belong to the family village somehow.

Our tour bus pulled into my Aunt Debbie's and Uncle Bobby's home around 8:30 pm. I never understood how we were related, but I was told that they were family, and I didn't question it. They did not live in a mansion, but they had enough space for our great party of 10. Actually, they did not have enough space for a normal family, but we liked to be crammed tightly into each other's personal space like puppies.

The next day we went to the family reunion. My father reintroduced us to cousins that we would never remember, and we sat at a table amongst ourselves. At the end of the evening my father clued us in on his secret mission.

"Looks like we are going to have breakfast tomorrow with your grandfather."

We buried my PaPa almost 10 years ago. "Your real dad is going to have breakfast with us?" I said in disbelief. My father told me that he met me and Keith when we were little and the twins met him as well, but they didn't recall the encounter either.

I had a restless night trying to figure out what role I would play in this visit that I didn't fully understand. My father was in his mid 50's, and he was still struggling to build a relationship with his biological father. I grew up with my PaPa, and I never had to struggle to build a relationship with PaPa, and as far as I was concerned my father's dad was not alive. But because this man was important to my dad, I decided to treat him with respect. I vaguely remember a time in which we were supposed to meet him, and he stood us up. I think my Granny cursed him out and this breakfast better proceed as planned our else I am going to break open another box of tampons on my daddy's behalf.

We pulled into the IHOP. Only my immediate family was present. My hoodself said, "We gotta meet this man at the IHOP cuzz we the jump off family. Dis is some bull." All nine of us sat at the table together. I sat right next to Grandpa Such and Such. I determined that I would treat him like a business client that I met for the first time.

"You sure have a good looking family." Grandpa Such and Such said. I hoped that he did not secretly take any credit for my dad's beautiful family. Grandpa Such and Such was a nice looking elderly man. I could tell that he was extremely attractive in his youth.

"So what do you like to do?" I knew that this question was general, but it would take me to other places so I listened with curious eyes.

"Ever since I retired, I spend most of my time at my church. I am on several boards, and it keeps me busy." Hmm a church going man that did not even have the heart to go to his own son's funeral. My

Uncle Daryl passed away at the age of 45, and he did not even send a card, but I didn't say anything negative, I just smiled.

"What industry did you retire from?"

"I retired from the Postal Service. I was the postmaster, and I did the majority of the hiring and firing." Well woop de do is what I really wanted to say, but I just kept smiling.

My father interjected and rambled off a series of my sibling's accomplishments, and I wanted to yell *"Daddy we don't have to impress this Nigga. He should try and impress us."*

"I used to interview a lot of people, and I can tell a lot about people from talking to them. I can tell that you are successful because you are very inquisitive. You are a school teacher right?" He looked at me.

"No, I am a retired school teacher. I retired after two strong years of dedicated service. I am in sales now, and it goes with my social butterfly personality."

"Are you married?"

"No." I said unapologetically.

"Maybe if you weren't such a social butterfly then you would be married." Oh now he dun messed with the church's money. It is on. I knew what my father wanted. He wanted a chance to meet his brothers and sisters on his dad's side of the family, and he wanted to be included. My father wanted to be recognized as part of the Such and Such family. My father wanted to keep the lines of communication open between him and his father so he never pushed the envelope, but I decided to throw the envelope in the post master's face.

"Did you pledge a fraternity in undergraduate school?" I strategically asked a few benign questions only to set him up for the malignant ones.

"Yes, I am a man of Alpha Phi Alpha fraternity."

"Ahh, an Alpha man. I bet you were something else. So how did you meet Granny?" Everyone at the table looked at my father when

I asked this question to gauge his approval, and he gave a slight nod and we waited for the story.

"I was working as a porter for the trains, and I met your grandmother."

"My Granny looked good didn't she?"

"Yes and I didn't look bad myself."

"How long did you guys date?" I could tell that this question made him uncomfortable, but I didn't care.

"We were both married when we met." According to my grandmother this was a lie. She was divorced, and he was an unhappily married man that was madly in love with her. He was sleeping on the couch instead of sharing a bed with his wife. God bless his wife's soul. She passed away two years ago, and she had to be miserable living with a husband that slept on the couch for all those years.

I changed gears on the conversation. "Do any of your children know about my father?" I asked and his hands began to shake. He must have developed acute Parkinson's syndrome.

"No."

"If you told any of your children, which one would it be?" Everyone flashed a look at my father again, and he gave his nod of approval.

"Kenneth." He replied and took a huge gulp of water.

"Who would have the hardest time dealing with the situation?"

"I don't think that anyone would have a hard time dealing with it. Their mother has passed on, and my kids would eventually be ok." I decided to cool off the conversation before it destructed.

"Do you have any pictures of your grandkids?"

"Yes." He pulled out pictures of young adults in in their early 20's.

"So when do we get to meet them?" I knew that the conversation would be over shortly after this question, but I was over Grandpa Such and Such anyway.

"Baby Steps first. Baby steps. Your father will be the first to meet them." His hands were waving at the table in front him uncontrollably.

"What will be the best month for him to meet them?" My dad looked at me with a new eye of respect.

"Baby Steps. Baby Steps." Was his only reply and I folded myself into the chair and rested my cheek in the palm of my hand in a Shirley Templish posture.

"You do realize that your baby is 53."

He looked at his watch and took another gulp of water.

"Can you send us pictures of yourself and your children?" I knew that breakfast was over.

"Yes, I will email them to your father."

"Look at you! You use an email account?" I asked in a high pitched tone

"Oh Yes! That is how I communicate with my church members." He said proudly.

We debriefed in the car, and I had earned stripes on my big sister coat of armor. My father was satisfied, and so was I.

A few months had passed, and he still had not sent the pictures that he promised.

For this I Give You Praise

CASSIDY'S LUNGS WERE no match for the pollen in the air. I'm not sure why human beings evolved to develop a severe reaction to one of nature's best performances, but the show brought tears to everyone in my household. Every day in April that I did not have to go to the emergency room to treat Cassidy's asthma was a good day. And every Sunday that I decided to go to a real church instead of the First Baptist Couch of Christ was a good week. This would be a start to a good one.

"If you want to get a seat at church you better hurry up," Erin warned me. This Sunday was a special occasion for Friendly Temple Missionary Baptist Church, it was the last day of service for the old church and Reverend Al Sharpton was coming to the church to commemorate the occasion.

"Hey Girl, I am walking out of the house now. Wait for us because I know that parking is going to be a beast, and it will be easier if we go in one car."

"OK, I'm putting on my makeup now, and once I'm finished I'm rolling out." I knew that this meant that Erin was probably still in her robe, and I would have plenty enough time to make it to her house.

For once we were on time for church and on this occasion, it meant we were probably too late. When we made it to the Sanctuary, which was actually in the gymnasium of the church, all of the seats were almost filled. I was not an actual member of Friendly Temple. I just flirted with the congregation from time to time. My grandparent's home was only a short walk from the church, and I was proud of how the church had the power to influence one of the most defunct areas in the west side of St. Louis.

Because of the layout of the gymnasium you could see everyone that entered the building, and there was perpetual motion. It made my spirit restless. People were constantly moving around the gymnasium as the choir belted out notes of praise. My living room was more peaceful, and this was one of my favorite excuses for attending The First Baptist Couch of Christ in my living room. However, this year had started pretty rocky, and I needed an altar to call on. I became a frequent visitor at Friendly Temple and on most Sundays I ignored the excuses.

Pastor Mike Jones made the announcement that Reverend Al Sharpton was in the building and welcomed him into the pull pit. The energy of the congregation shifted to stillness as Reverend Al Sharpton and his entourage marched to the stage. We all were familiar with the public perception of Al Sharpton. I read his book, and it should be a required reading for high school social studies. He basically explained how he committed political suicide for the civil rights of the people.

I looked over at Cassidy. She was watching and listening with her eyes. I was so happy to share this moment with my daughter. Cody was only three years old, and I knew that he was not listening, but I knew that there would be a day that he will mature, and he will be proud that he was there. I felt like my mom in a slightly thinner version. She made her entire parenting career all about exposure, and she exposed us to literature, religions, and politics in her own special way.

Reverend's message was inspiring to the inspirable, and to the lost souls of the building, it was time served for a lucky chance into heaven. Al Sharpton preached from John 5:1-9. In this text, Jesus went into Bethesda and came into a crowd of people suffering from blindness, sickness and lameness. The people were all waiting for the angels to trouble the waters so that they could be healed. In this text a crippled man sat on the banks of a pool of water for 38 years waiting for his chance to get into the water. Jesus asked the man, "Do you want to be made whole?" The man replied with an excuse instead of a simple yes and he told Christ that, "He didn't have a man to carry him into the water. Then Jesus commanded the man to "Rise, take up thy bed and walk," and the man was made whole.

At this moment, during this sermon, I asked myself did I want to be made whole. I replied, "Yes." And I gave God the glory for everything in my life that he had already blessed me with, and I said to myself, "I don't need a man to carry me into the water." "I am whole." But in the middle of the night when my kids are sound asleep, I am all alone. My flesh burns and for that I need a man. It's no other way around it. Well, it's a few ways around it, but I'm sure that those routes can be condemned as well.

Should I envy or pity the young single women of the church who proudly say that they have not been with a man in years? I envy them. I envy them like recovering alcoholics envy a bar full of social drinkers. So, on second thought maybe I'm not whole. It is now April and I have not been with a man since February, and I am right around my tipping point. Asexuality is not a lifestyle that I can endorse and there is not a single commandment that says that I have to. "*Do you want to be made whole?*" I would have been married years ago, if Ryan would have proposed, and I would not have had to wait by the water with the rest of the sexually immoral citizens of the world. "*Rise, take up thy bed and walk.*" I don't even understand what that means for me and my life.

Service ended with Reverend Al Sharpton calling for the community to increase our vigilance in local politics. Overall, it was inspiring. At the end, I dropped my tithes and offering envelope in the bucket like a raffle ticket. Heaven help me!

What About Us

FIVE MONTHS PASSED since the infamous cake protest. The protest marked an all-time emotional low point for me and the end of the romantic relationship that I shared with Ryan. I can't imagine getting back into a relationship with him, and it's even harder to imagine my entire life without him. Perhaps my love for Ryan is an addiction. After I succumb to the desire to be in Ryan's arms again, will cravings develop? Will I go through the stages of a love spree to include regret and another firm resolution to never love him again emerging remorseful with a firm resolution to never love him again? Our conversations grew more personal for two weeks, and I felt what was coming next. I might drink again.

Erin and I talked on the telephone daily. Our telephone daily conflicts could all be solved by a solution to the he loves me so he loves me not riddle. What a waste of two brilliant minds. We could be talking about solving an infinite amount of neighborhood, state, or union affairs. The justification of love dominated our lives and time.

My journey to a small town called Taylorville in southern Illinois felt like a trip to the end of the earth, and to past the time, we ran our engines and our mouths.

"Look bestie, I am on team Jazzmine. If you want to get back with Ryan, I support you 100 percent, but do you think you will be happy?"

"I don't know about how happy I will be, but single parenting is hard, and I don't want to go through what I have gone through with Cassidy. When Cody goes to school, I don't want to do it all alone, all over again."

"Well, let me throw this out there. Ryan and Chris are two different people. Ryan will always be active in Cody's life, and you will not have the same experience as you had with Cassidy." I was usually the voice of reason, but on this call, Erin assumed the responsibility.

"That's true, and I know things will not be as difficult they are with Cassidy and her father. I know that I will not have to raise Cody alone, but if there is a chance that our family can work together, if there is a chance that weekdays, weekends, and holidays don't have to be split, then I want to take the chance."

"I hear you, but you deserve more, J.....real talk. What about you?"

"I will be fine. Ryan isn't abusive. He's just dismissive. He is a great father, and there isn't a perfect man in the world. So the devil that I know is better than the devil that I don't know."

I had conversations like this with my mother, my aunt Lynn, my second mother Lisa, Miss Jennifer at the daycare, and everyone else that had ears. They were not true conversations. I was not looking for answers. The conversations were opportunities for me to convince myself that despite everything that I had already went through with Ryan I should try one more time. I should put my heart on the line again for the sake of my family.

My mother's response was encouraging. My mother fell in love with spirits, and she felt in her heart that Ryan had a good spirit. And for this reason, he was worth the emotional risk. Aunt Lynn, Lisa, and Miss Jennifer were categorically against the idea. In their own way they all said that I was everything a man would love and hope for in a woman, and I needed to only take an emotional risk for a man that was everything that a woman would love and hope for in a man. It made perfect sense, but in my heart, I had already marginalized my expectations for love. The love that I give is never reciprocated, but it is always reminisced.

My Friday happy hour consisted of watching movies with Cody and Cassidy and taking a long hot bubble bath while the kids stayed up later than usual watching kid sitcoms. I pinned my hair in a bun and tied a scarf around my head so the bubbles would not get my hair wet. The Bose speaker sat on the bathroom floor, and my Anthony Hamilton playlist worked its magic. My heartbeat and breath danced with every musical note. The smell of the eucalyptus candle caressed the air, and I was in a zone. My chi was exactly where it needed to be. Not too loose and not too tight. This position, this asana, lasted for 15 invigorating minutes, and then I heard my daughter yelling.

"Momma! Momma! Mom!"

"What?" I yelled hoping that I could fulfill her needs without leaving the bathtub so that I could quickly get back into my pose.

"You need to come downstairs. It is serious." I could tell by her voice that something was broken or ruined. I hoped they did not break my television.   I put on a towel and ran downstairs, with water still dripping from my body. I didn't want to dry off completely because that would be an admission to myself that I would not be returning to the bubble bath, and I was not ready to give that up. I looked at Cassidy's face, and it was stern and mature as if she was my mother and about to put me in my place. Then I looked down and saw my pink purple pearl shaded vibrator in her hand.

"Your son was playing with this." She slammed the obviously penis shaped object into my hands. I pressed my lips together as tight as they could get and opened my eyes as wide as they could open, grabbed the object, and turned exactly 180 degrees and walked away.

Last night I attempted to hide my rabbit under the bed. I didn't expect Cody to go under my bed to play. My hiding spot was pretty lame, and I decided to move it to a hard to reach shoebox. I was not ready to part ways with my rabbit. We had a good thing going. After listening to Anthony Hamilton and chilling in the bathtub,

I was considering changing my last name to rabbit as a matter of fact.

"Mommy, Mommy." Cody showed up in my room just as I hid my special friend. His face was drenched in tears.

"What's the matter baby?"   My embarrassed expression was replaced with one of worry.

"I want da bop-it back." My son had confused my vibrator with the pull-it, pass-it, flick-it, turn-it Hasbro Bop It toy. The thought of my two and a half year old son pulling and tugging on my special friend was purely disgusting. His imagination was hilarious, and I laughed so hard tears rolled down my cheeks.

"Cody, it's gone." I did not try to explain that it was mommy's toy and not his. He peaked in the small trash can in my room and underneath the bed. "Cody, it's gone buddy. You have more toys in your room." He left my room disappointed at the loss of his newly discovered toy, and I laid still on my bed wondering what I should say to my daughter. I chose to not discuss it at all. My daughter was 12, and I was neither ready to have the masturbation talk with her at this time nor could I call up my mother and ask her how to have this discussion.

It was after 10 o'clock, and my cell phone rang. I looked at the name. It was Ryan. Over the past few weeks we had met for lunch a few times, and throughout the day we would talk on the phone. He kept his same schedule with Cody, and we never talked at night.

"Hello." I said softly

"Hey, I am driving through the city from Festus. I have been working since 4:30 am on a property near Caruthersville, MO. Is it ok if I stay at your place tonight? I will make a pallet on the floor in Cody's room. I just don't want to drive all the way home."

"Yeah right."

"I'm serious. We don't have to do nothing."

Ryan showed up 15 minutes later. A pallet was never made, and something was done.

Purple Reign

SATURDAY'S SUNSHINE HID behind the soft gray storm clouds. The rain splashed seductively on the window pane, and I opened my eyes and caught Ryan's gaze in the act.

"Good Morning." Ryan let out a breath of relief. Our months apart began to worry him, and we were both relieved that our break up period was now over.

"Good Morning. I thought you said you were going to make a pallet in Cody's room. Why the hell are you in my bed?"

"Shit you attacked me. I was scared to leave your room." This remark was funny and embarrassingly true.

"Whatever. I don't know what you are talking about. Are you hungry?"

"Not really. I never eat this early in the morning."

"Well, I am going to go downstairs and make breakfast. I am starving."

"After last night, I am sure you are." I gave him a look. That you know what it is look and walked away.

I made the Saturday morning usual pancakes, eggs, and bacon. I brewed coffee and returned upstairs. I handed Ryan a full plate and made a second trip downstairs to get my plate and my coffee.

"Jazzmine, I'm ready."

"Ready for what?" I asked.

"To do the whole deal." I assumed this was his way of saying that he was ready to get married. I did not want to leave anything for interpretation so I asked a clarifying question.

"What exactly does do the whole deal mean?"

"I am ready for us to be a complete family. I want to get married. You are a great girl, and you deserve a respectful life. I hate that you have to be burdened by situations that I caused, and I don't want it to be like that for us anymore. I am growing up. I have a son, and I want things to be right."

"So is this your way of asking me to marry you?" My face did not look anything like the faces of the women from the Jared Galleria of Jewelry commercials, so I knew that this was not an official proposal. This was more like a post-pre-proposal.

"No, I am going to show you this time, that I am serious."

"Ok, we will see, but I am used to you suggesting that we will get married soon. We always get pre-engaged, but I never get a ring." Verbally, I committed to another round of loving Ryan, and it is what I wanted to do, but I wanted him to know that I was serious about a true commitment. I wanted to get married. He was not going to continue to keep eating my pancakes for nothing.

From that day on we continued our relationship as if it had never stopped. We made family plans for the weekend and carried on like we had carried on for the last seven years of knowing each other. On the weekends, we fumbled with recipes for exotic steak flavors and sipped wine as we watched the kids play and fight. Our life together was great.

Unlike other times that we reunited, this time, I made a deal with myself to continue to build and enjoy the life that I created without Ryan. To my close girlfriends, I was the friend that appeared when her boo thang disappeared, and I would fall off the activity scene when I fell back in love, but I continued my occasional happy hours. I remained active in my professional organizations and attended every National Sales Network meeting.

My clients were always inquisitive about my family life. I did not disclose the details of our break up after the cake incident, but I did inform everyone that asked that Ryan and I were no longer together. I made the decision to leave things that way so that I would no longer have to discuss my relationship with my clients even though we were trying to make things work again. The next announcement I would make about Ryan would be regarding our engagement. Other than that, I will not bring up his name.

Being with Ryan did not feel like happiness, it fell like complacency with the potential of happiness. The romantic love that I shared with him had slipped from my heart to my appendix, and I wanted him to earn his way back to a spot in my heart.

• • •

Life was so much smoother with Ryan around. Ryan's work schedule was still hectic, but he seemed to squeeze in a little time for us.

"What are your plans for the weekend?

"I really didn't have any."

"Ben just moved into a new home in University City, and he wanted to invite us over for dinner on Saturday."

"That's fine. What do we need to bring?"

"I want to broil beef tenderloin. I will call him and let him know that it is a go." I have known Ben since junior high school. In school, his notes were always very meticulous, and he kept a well-organized leather like agenda that I mimicked. It was something about looking over his shoulder and seeing fine print on each day of the month that impressed me. At 12 years old, Ben Newman had a clear agenda, and it had paid off big time. Ryan and Ben were an odd friend match, but there was a mutual respect for their hard work, ambition, and a love for basketball that cemented their relationship.

Our dinner with Ben and Amy, his wife was scheduled for 4:00 sharp. Ben and Amy were not colored people nor did they operate on colored people's time. I prepped the ingredients for the tenderloin rub and Ryan called me in the midst.

"Is Cody dressed and ready to go? I will pull into your house at 3:00 on the dot, and we need to be ready to roll out. You know that I hate to be late." He said this as if I loved to be late, and he never considered how much I have to multi-task during the course of the day. Between my kids, career, my man, and friends, my life was always quadruple booked.

"I know that you want to get there on time, and we are ready to go. Did you remember to bring the meat thermometer from your house?" Last Sunday Ryan prepared dinner for me and his mother at his home, and he borrowed my meat thermometer.

"Shit, I forgot it and I won't have time to go back and get it."

"I guess we have to make do without it." This situation frustrated me more than I let on. It was a reminder of how even the little things in our life are complicated because of our situation. Even though our reunion was barely approaching six weeks, I wondered how long this would continue.

We arrived at Ben's house at 4:00 pm sharp looking like an all American African- American family. The home was situated in an Orthodox Jewish neighborhood. The streets and most of the lights were out on the block in honor of the Sabbath. Our color schemes of our attire were well matched, and our faces were polished happy.

"Benji, Hello." I always greeted Ben by his childhood name. I believed that I remembered Ben from the kindergarten program at the Ladue Early Childhood Center. I remembered that we called him Benji. There was also a little boy that gave me a gray toy car that he was no longer playing with. I used that car for my Barbie dolls until I was 13 years old. The car came from a little boy name Benji from the childhood center, but I never could confirm that it was Ben, and of course, he wouldn't remember.

I remembered the event because it was one of my first exchanges with a little person that didn't share the same skin color as I did. As I grew older, I realized that there was a fear of interracial interactions, but as an adult, I never developed those anxieties.   Perhaps it was because I received my first car from a white little boy with brown curly hair.

"What's going on Ryan?"

"Hard work and low wages." Ben smiled at Ryan's classic response. I tried to talk to Ryan about speaking situations into existence, and he simply challenged the conversation, but it was slowly becoming his reality.

"Jazzmine, you've met Amy."

"Yes. " I turned to Amy and said hello. Amy and Ben made an extremely handsome couple; if they did not introduce themselves as husband and wife you would have assumed they were brother and sister.

"Where is Isaac?" Isaac was the exact same age as Cody. Ryan and Ben had brought the boys together on several occasions, but this was my first time meeting him. Isaac peeked his head around the kitchen counter, and he looked exactly like the little boy that gave me the gray toy car.

"Oh my goodness, Ben, he looks like your little mini-me."

"You think? He looks like Amy to me."

"You two look so much alike, I really can't say."

"So, Amy how is work going?"

"Work is keep me very busy. The buyout has changed everything for our department." I wasn't totally sure of Amy's role at Anheuser Busch, but she was pretty high on the food chain. The Newman's were neither hurting for cash nor were they arrogantly flaunting it.

"Amy, let's give them a tour of the house." Ben led the tour. Amy propped Isaac on her hip, and I picked up Cody and positioned him on my hip as well. We walked up a beautiful staircase lined with a decorative wrought iron railing, and into a sitting area transformed into a playroom for Isaac. Cody was drawn to this space immediately, and we put the children down and let them have at it.

"This is really nice. I love the granite in the bathrooms." I noticed the master's suite had a space dedicated to Ben's watches. I really wanted to say, "Damn Ben, you doing it like that?" But I kept it to myself.

Dinner was ready, and we all met at the table. The food sat in the middle of the table and we took our places around it. I sat to the left of Amy and on the right side of history. Our talk was small and of little consequence, but if Martin Luther King and Sarah Palin could have been there, we could have solved all of the nation's domestic issues. Martin would have been the perfect mediator to the discussion and Sarah could have acquired the missing link to her understanding of the keel of America. Since they didn't show up, we passed the time with idle chat about sports and work. The conversations became a little more intimate when we discussed our children, but it would be nice if a forum like this could be used to discuss politics. The Newman's are ruby red republicans and for reasons as solid as Condoleezza Rice's. The Jones-Justice-Swans were as blue as a sapphire for reasons as solid as Reverend Jesse Jackson's.

Newman could argue me to the cows came home about self-reliance and religion and after he spoke his very first sentence, I would agree. I would agree with the second sentence and the third. The majority of his statements would probably go uncontested. I love the Lord, my country, and my independence. Newman and I were educated in the same tradition but our life started at different marks. Newman knows the well to do African-Americans and in his heart he knows that we can all reach that point if we will ourselves to it, but he underestimates the number of bullets that we have to dodge to protect our hearts to achieve that end. Those bullets require the intervention of the federal and local government.

I looked over at Ryan. His hands moved at a faster pace and his conversation spun in circles. Ryan was obviously uneasy at the table not because of the luxury of the home nor the wealth of our host.

Maybe he was nervous to be in a household in which the women could hold down the fort, but the man was man enough to not force her to.

I secretly wished that I could insert a syringe into Ben's leg and draw whatever blood that made him accept Jesus, love his wife, and protect his family the way that he did. I would then squirt that blood right into Ryan and live happily ever after.

All or Nothing

RYAN'S PARENTS ANNOUNCED they were getting a divorce after 33 years of marriage. A few months went by, and all we discussed was the heat, rain, and the progression of Ryan's parents' divorce. Spring's beautiful blossoms were overlooked, and the summer heat started to settle in.

There was never a smooth way to transition into a conversation about us. As we watched the local news on the couch, we made small talk about the St. Louis murder count, insurgent attacks in the Middle East, and I went for it.

"When should I plan to go to the jeweler? Will it be before or after Cody graduates from high school?"

"You got jokes. I have already made an appointment for Tuesday after you get off from work if that works with your schedule."

"I can make it." *You damn right I can.* After work, I met Ryan at a small jeweler in downtown Clayton. A sweet Jewish couple owned and operated the quaint shop. I eyed all of the beautiful jewelry. Engagement rings were only a small section of the offerings. Each case was filled with a statement piece that says he-loves-me-so. We had gone through hell just to make it to the engagement case, so I don't know what I would have to go through to get something out of the he-loves-me-so case.

I tried on ring after ring until I found the perfect stone. It was a tear drop shaped diamond slightly under two carats in an antique setting.

"This is the one." I admired it quickly and looked over at Ryan.

"Alright, how much is this going to set me back?" He asked the wife. She discreetly showed him the price and his response was, "Emmm," Like he had just swallowed a shot of hard liquor.

"This is the one you want huh?"

"Yes, it's beautiful."

"I want you to look at one more store, and I will go from there."

We went to the other jewelry store and found a ring that I liked a little. It was almost an emerald cut stone, and it was placed in an antique setting.

I was so excited to finally ring shop. This had to mean something. In all of our years together, he had never taken me to shop for rings.

Ryan and I parted ways, and I couldn't wait to call someone and tell them that we had finally looked at engagement rings. I dialed my mother, no answer. I called my Aunt Lynn.

"Whatcha know good?" She answered in a cheerful voice.

"Guess what Auntie."

"What?" She did not make an attempt to guess.

"Me and Ryan went ring shopping."

"Oh, OK." She responded dryly.

"I found a beautiful ring. It was a tear drop shaped diamond in an antique setting. It was purty."

"Well, let me know when he proposes. I will believe the ring is purty when I see it."

"He's going to propose soon."

"He better. It looks like he just pulled the oldest trick in the book if you wanna know the truth."

"What trick?"

"Girl, his ass is just buying time. He noticed that you weren't paying him any attention so he had to put his feet back in the door. Now that he has showed you a few rings, he got another six months to act a damn fool."

I wanted to take up for Ryan, but he had let me down so many times before. So I just listened and said, "We will see."

The next morning during my drive to drop off Cody at day care I called as many people as I could to tell them the mediocre news. All of the responses were lackluster. I spared my dad because I was certain that he would feel just as his sister, Lynn, did.

I walked into Cody's day care and spotted a real face to share the news with.

"Jennifer, guess what I did yesterday?"

"Whatchu do girl?" Her voice lowered and her ears anticipated a juicy story.

"Ryan and I went shopping for engagements rings."

"For what?" *What kind of response was that?* Jennifer had been there for me during a lot of low moments with Ryan and I thought she would be happy that we were making strides towards marriage.

"So that he can buy a ring and ask me to marry him...duh?"

"I hope he does not buy that ring because you are not going to be happy. You deserve more, Jazz. You deserve someone who will treat you right, and this marriage will only be great for Cody and Ryan. You will need a boyfriend if you marry that man. Your spirit is so different from his. Money wise he does his thing, but your personality is here and his personality is there." She put one hand significantly higher than the other to illustrate her point.

"He ain't that bad Jennifer, and it's better to deal with the devil that you know than the one that you don't know."

"Whoever told you that lied to you. Stop dealing with devils Jazz, and have a good day at work." She curled her lips and followed me out the door..

"Oh Jennifer, I want to remind you. I will be in California next week for work."

"Have some fun for me." She shut the iron screened door.

Go Go

THE FLIGHT WAS smooth, and I spent the majority of it reading articles from medical journals and reviewing marketing materials for the test that would follow the four day training session. I walked into the lobby and checked in with the receptionist.

"Have a great day Miss Steele. Would you like assistance with your bags?"

"Yes please. Has my roommate checked in?"

"It shows in our system that you are rooming with Kelsey Mitchum, and at this time, she has not arrived."

"Thank You." I passed several familiar faces along the way and unlike most pharmaceutical companies. A lot of the familiar faces were brown. This phenomenon made my company extremely unique, and it also made company meetings adventurous.

I made it to my room and chose the bed by the window. My body flopped onto the bed and took five intoxicating deep breaths. Before I allowed myself to get too comfortable, I searched for the room service menu. This was a big deal for me. In all my years of travel as a child and young adult, I never had the habit or ability to order room service, and now that I was a "professional" it was an absolute necessity. I could have grabbed lunch at one of the eateries in the lobby, but they were always crowded and full of corporate bodies. This would be one of the few opportunities that I would have alone.

In the middle of my private lunch, I heard someone at the door.

"Hey Girl." Kelsey and all of her luggage fell into the room at once.

"Well, hello my southern bell." Kelsey removed her Chanel sunglasses and placed them into a matching sunglass case. "I don't know why they are taking us out of the field for four days. It is not like the company has any new information to present. Have you checked in at the registration desk yet?" Kelsey's Valentino stilettos paced the floor and gave her arms marching orders to unpack.

"No, I have been stuffing my face." I dipped two French fries into a mound of ketchup and took a swig of my coke on the rocks.

"You have the diet of a college student. I don't see how you do it." I was a full size six. Kelsey was unsatisfied at a size four and content with being a size two. "Let's go down and register. The general session starts in 30 minutes. I applied a little lip gloss, dusted my face with a little pressed powder, and we cat walked down the hall.

"When we get back to the room, we have to catch up. Oh and I have to tell you about my birthday trip in Italy." Kelsey was my corporate America big sister. She had been in the game for a while, and she knew exactly how to win. She was a straight shooter and suspicious of everything and everybody. I learned so much from her. I believed her draw to me was my flightiness and my ability to do something that she could only dream of and that was to go with the flow.

General session was held in an auditorium in the convention area of the hotel. Before I made my way to join my colleagues from my region, I grabbed snacks and a bottled beverage from a table in the lobby of the auditorium. I didn't really want them, but they were free so why not.

I entered a different realm of corporate America as I walked through the entrance way. The sounds and lyrics from the Black Eyed Peas' hit song, *I Gotta Feeling* blasted through the speakers. Sales professionals from all across the country shuffled and shimmied to find their seats. I found a seat next to my team mate Collin.

"Hey J, I saved you a seat." J was my professional name, and it suited my sassy, to the point corporate persona.

"Are you ready for four days of this?" Collin was not a fan of being away from home.

"If it was just sitting and listening to the music, I would be fine, but the breakout sessions with role plays and listening to a bunch of people try and justify their jobs, I can do without."

The music lowered and then my favorite piece of eye candy came to the stage to present information from the marketing department. He graced the stage, Burberry clad from head to toe with a royal posture to match. His bright white smile was the perfect contrast to his milk dud polished skin. I am sure his presentation was delivered with conviction, but I didn't hear it. His words were Charlie Brown muted, and my imagination flew into the gutter.

"Hey J, you wanna grab a bite after general session." My partnership with Collin had truly surmounted all of my expectations. After four months of communicating, planning and meeting, we had become friends. My family situation was foreign to him, but instead of treating me like a baby momma, he faulted Ryan. I brought him up to speed on the educated black man, and how they approached committed relationships differently from men from other cultures. In so many words, he let me know that he placed Ryan in the bucket for the weak and mentally unstable, and he respected me and held conversations with me as if I was both a man and a woman.

"Yes, I think Morgan made reservations for all of us to go to a restaurant off site." Our team was an unruly mismatched bunch, unlike other teams that were uniform and plain boring. As a team we respected each other's professionalism and work ethic, but at dinner we let our locs down.

We arrived at a modern chop house known for the high quality cuts of beef. Collectively, the group compared notes on who had the nuttiest clients. Morgan told a story about how a team mate drove on a shut down highway while she was riding in the passenger seat. We had several new people to our team and Morgan loved to share the story of how she discovered me at Starbucks. It was true, I was her favorite barista, and that lead me to a job offer.

"Would you like me to bring the check?" The waiter asked.

"Yes, we're ready. Did anyone want coffee?" There were a few takers and the waiter returned with coffee and the check.

"Wait. Wait." I wanted to play the check game and held the black book with the check concealed in it. "Does everyone know how to play the check game?"

"Yes, the game where we all put in five dollars and the person who guesses the amount of the check wins." Alison answered. Everyone put their money in the center of the table and the grand prize was around $60. Everyone wrote a number on a slip of paper and waited anxiously for the grand total of the check.

"The grand total is $1,874." I called out. Everyone yelled out a number most of them were well below the actual dollar amount. Another member of the team yelled, "I wrote $1800." He reached for the money, and I turned over my paper, and it was $1850.

I grabbed the wad of cash and the words, "yeah bitches," slid out of my mouth before I could put them back in. There was a clear and obvious moment of silence at the table.

Then Morgan said," Did you guys hear that? Yeah bitches? Did Jazzmine just say "yeah bitches? Let's all get cigars."

I heard "yeah bitches" a dozen times from just about everyone on the team before we left the restaurant.

We found a small cigar bar and smoked cigars and sipped wine. This was a great way to end a very long day.

I came into the room to find Kelsey sound asleep. I tried my best to not make any noise and fell into a deep sleep.

I woke up feeling refreshed and odd. I didn't have to get anyone ready for school nor did I have to drop anyone off at daycare, but that was part of my jumpstart to my day. Overall, I felt good and slightly guilty for enjoying the fact that I could just think of myself for the morning.

The day before, I hung all of my clothes in the hotel closet. This was something that I did only because I noticed that Kelsey did it whenever we would room together at company meetings. One would be able to distinguish Kelsey's side of the closet from Jazzmine's. Her closet did not have an article of clothing with color in it and my side had colors from every season. After looking at her side of the closet, I made a mental note to tone things down a little bit in my wardrobe. I wanted a universal look, and my style was leaning more on the St. Louis Chic side of the scale. As a side note, St. Louis was recognized as one of the worst dress cities on an internet poll.

Whatever I wore, it must have looked good on me because I turned the heads of everybody in my small training session. It was nothing over the top. It was a pale yellow form fitting dress with a white collared dickey and navy stilettos. Kelsey told me that I looked like a naughty kindergarten teacher, and I just laughed.

"Good morning everyone. Take a look around. You should see a lot of unfamiliar faces. We wanted to mix you guys up so that you can have the opportunity to share best practices from colleagues that you don't talk to everyday. So, to get things warmed up. I want everyone to introduce themselves. Tell us how long you have been with the company and your first concert that you ever attended." I hated the introduction game, but I appreciated the new twist at the end. I would never remember all of the names or how many years a person was at the company, but it would be interesting to hear the answer to the concert question.

Bon Jovi was yelled out several times and the crowd said "nice." I was happy to know that there were three colleagues that called out Michael Jackson as their first concert performance. I had something in common with at least three people in the room. It took an hour for 50 people to run through the introduction. I wished that this exercise would adjourn this session, but it was only the beginning.

There were videos and live lectures from a manager in a territory out of Tennessee. I loved the soothing accent, but I felt it rocking me to sleep. He reached out to the audience for help whenever he noticed that he had lost the crowd, and all I could think of is that a screenwriter from Saturday Night Live could leave a really good mark with this scene.

The morning sessions ended, and lunch began. The afternoon sessions began, and during an afternoon break, I migrated to a circle of familiar faces.

"Hey, J how have you been? You're looking nice." Double fisted with a bag of chips in one hand and a fruit and cheese plate in the other, I reached to give a colleague from Texas a hug. It took me years to remember his real name, but we would always call him Rosé, the alias of Rick Ross. His stomach could not compare to Rick Ross' by no stretch, but he had a full beard and his complexion was similar to the rapper's, and that is how he earned the name.

"Thanks Rosé. What's been good in your world?"

"Can't call it. Just tryin to maintain." After sitting in the breakout sessions and being away from home for almost two days we couldn't wait to speak in our other dialect.

"That's what's up." I put a few pita chips next to a spoonful of hummus.

"I wanted to let you in on something. A group of us decided to rent a party bus and go into LA tonight. Let me know if you want to roll. Don't mention it to anyone else because there are only a limited amount of seats. Just let me know if you want in."

"Oh yeah, I'm in, but we have the company dinner tonight. How are we going to pull that one off?"

"We will show our faces, pay our respects, then bounce." Anticipating the evening events gave my mind something to focus on as I blankly stared at the manager from Tennessee, and the videos that we had to watch for the rest of the afternoon. After they were over, I met Collin for my first round of drinks for the evening.

"What do you have planned after the reception?" My life was intriguing to him especially during company away meetings. He knew that Ryan and I were back together, but he wanted to believe that I was taking advantage of the opportunity of being a single woman in an atmosphere of attractive people of all shades of color.

"Nothing I may go to the room and rent a movie. Did you know that you could rent movies that were showing at the theatre?"

"Don't even try and pull that shit with me. You ain't going to your room and watch a damn movie. Now, tell me J. What are you getting into?" Collin called me out, and I looked like the little sister that had just got caught in a lie.   In fact if I had a big brother who was white from a rural small town who loved Nascar racing and the republican tea party, it would be Collin.

"Ok, alright, a group of reps rented a party bus, and we are going to kick it in LA."

"Put it right here." He held out his hand for me to high five it. Are you going to have any after-hours fun?"

"Collin, I don't get my meat where I make my bread." He laughed, and we gulped down our drinks and headed to the reception.

The theme of the reception was an Asian bistro extravaganza. There were Chinese lanterns throughout the garden area of the hotel. Waitresses dressed as Geishas passed out hors d'oeuvres.

"I would like a glass of pinot noir please." I chose this over a cabernet sauvignon or a merlot because I hated the way red wine stained my lips.

"J, are you ready for what's about to happen?" He bucked his eyes and sipped his scotch.

"Yes, I'm ready."

"No, are you ready? Rosé got the brown and white liquor on deck. This party bus is about to be everything." I hadn't given it much thought, but the way my colleague hyped up the event made me say my corporate hellos and goodbyes at a faster pace.

"We have 10 minutes before the bus leaves. We better make our way there." I nodded and placed my empty glass on a nearby table.

"OK let's roll." We approached the black party bus. At first glance it looked like an ordinary black, brand new, oversized van.

I used my fist to pound on the door.

"Open the doh Negro." I wasn't sure where I picked up that line, but it had to be from some movie that I saw at some point in my life. Rosé opened the door and oh my! We were the last to get on the bus, and behind us there were two ladies that were turned away from the fun. Strobe lights illuminated the chairs and the faces of my fellow brown colleagues. A dancing pole rested in the middle of the bus towards the back end, and it was full of potential energy. T-Pain song, *I'm in love with a Stripper*, set the tone for dancing and without alcohol I cat walked toward the pole. I gripped the pole with my right hand and walked a complete 360 degrees around it. Leading with my head I went to the floor. Flicked my 18 inch head full of weave up and slowly returned to a standing position. I heard cheering from all angles of the bus and everyone started chanting "Ay...Ay...Ay." I cat walked back to my seat to found it occupied, so I took my place on a colleagues lap.

I was first to the pole, but I was not the last or the best. Another young lady started in on the pole just as I did. She kicked one leg up into the air and griped the pole with her leg she twirled and twirled releasing the stored energy and disseminating the kinetic energy into the crowd. Dollars flew into the air, and from there, it was on and popping.

We had all taken off our corporate girdles and sighed so hard on the dance floor. We could be ourselves. It's one thing that corporate America does not calculate the socialization process of being black in corporate America. It's a little easier if you were from a family of professionals, but that is usually not the case. Still to this date, we feel a certain way when more than three blacks congregate in a corporate setting. I have heard with my own ears black people say, "Ok, it's too many off us in one place. Time to break up the NAACP meeting." In the 21st century, I have heard black managers discuss how difficult it is to hire one of their own. Members from other racial groups never have to think like this. A white person never thinks about how to maneuver a crowd if he or she was the only white face there. That is a crowd that he or she would never make an appearance in because he or she wouldn't feel comfortable and that is the type of crowd that black folks greet every day.

The night of fun ended, and I returned to my room to find my roommate sound asleep. Kelsey was a sophisticate, and the party bus atmosphere would not have been a good look for her or so we all assumed. I called Ryan as a courtesy. I didn't expect him to answer the phone. It was 3:30 am in St. Louis. The purpose of dialing his number was to log in the call more than to talk. Then I drifted to sleep still shocked from the college-like fun we had all just experienced.

When I Wake Up

IT WAS THE middle of July and Cassidy spent the summer bonding with her father in Nashville. The upcoming school year would be her first year of middle school and a perfect time to transition to a new school. I was sick and tired of paying for private school, and I hoped that Ryan would propose before the end of the summer, and then we would move into his home, and she could go to the neighborhood school. This was a long, long, long shot so in between my sales calls. I searched the internet for more realistic options.

I finished up the work day and called Collin to relay a few business updates. Our partnership was good for business and our opportunities in our sales territory continued to expand.

"Hey, did you hear that Dr. Pullaski is no longer practicing at the hospital? I heard she was fired."

"Oh well, it wasn't like she helped us any. I hate to see someone lose their job, but she is a doctor. She will find another one. What are you getting into for the weekend?"

"Nothing, I am going to put some steaks on the grill and chill out tonight."

"You are going to grill! Wait a minute. I thought you and Ryan were hot and steamy again?"

"We're together. What does that have to do with me grilling?"

"He is supposed to do the grilling."

"Collin, he doesn't know how to grill."

"Wow, this fellow didn't have very many points with me, and I think he lost even more. What kind of man does not know how to grill?"

"Ryan."

"So every time you want barbecue you have to grill it yourself."

"No, sometimes my friend Toni grills, and I bring meat home."

"Does Ryan eat it?" His voice sounded like his face looked like we were talking about boogers.

"Yes." I said with hesitation.

"Oh, hell no. He shouldn't be eating some other man's meat." My eyes disappeared into my cheeks, I was laughing so hard, and I made a mental note to ask Toni to grill for me more often.

My condo had a spacious rooftop deck. A wicker love seat with taupe colored cushions occupied most of the space. I also had a teal blue bistro table that was a few feet away from the barbecue pit. I went through the motions of lighting the grill. While the charcoals blazed, I sat on the loveseat and sipped a cold glass of pinot grigio.

"Ryan. Ryan." I yelled, but I didn't get an answer. I went into the bedroom and looked into Cody's room. The house was so quiet. They must have left I thought. Parked on the street, I saw Ryan's car. The park was only an earshot away, and I could hear Cody yelling playfully at the park.

"I need to pick up some barbecue sauce from the grocery store. Will you watch the meat on the grill?" I used my inner-city voice waves to relay the message.

"Yeah, I got it."

In 10 minutes, I had everything that I needed from the store. The delay in returning home came in the check-out line. It was the first of the month, and everybody and their mommas were buying groceries. I stood in line for 30 minutes before I finally checked out. My trip to the grocery store to get wine and barbecue sauce was in vain because when I returned home all of my meat was burned to a crisp.

"I thought you said you were going to watch the meat."

"I checked on it a few minutes ago."

"It's all burned up. We can't even eat it. I didn't want you to watch it burn."

I made myself a sandwich and warmed a can of Spaghetti O's for Cody and called it a night.

That night, my attitude was all wrong for the occasion. I wanted to start some shit. "It's the middle of the summer, and I need to make plans to enroll Cassidy in school. Will she go to school from here or from your house?"

"I already know, Jazzmine. I know that you are not moving into my house without a ring. It's a few people that owe me a lot of money, and I need to collect it before I make any moves. I don't have a job in which I get paid a salary. The banks are not loaning money, and I need my cash in my hands to make moves."

"Ryan, if you saw a property that was $10,000, and you could profit $5,000, you would do whatever you needed to do to come up with that money, right?"

"Yes, where are you going with this?"

"I'm just sayin if you think something is a good deal, you make it happen. Maybe you don't think that us getting married is a good deal? You don't even bring it up."

Ryan started to speak as if he was a struggling reader, reading from a piece of paper. "Jazzmine, I want to marry you. I do not want to marry anyone else. I am not going anywhere. I am not avoiding conversations about marriage. It's nothing to talk about. It is something that I will do."

"Don't do me no motherfucking favors. If you want to continue on like this I don't know how long I'm going to follow your limp."

"I hate it when you get like this. Good night sweetheart." I didn't reply. I meditated on a postcard that I had received in the mail regarding a KIPP charter school.

I drifted asleep soundly despite the mini argument. Until Ryan's cell phone vibrated in the window sill. I could have been dreaming about a free shopping spree at the Chanel boutique off of 5th Avenue, but if that cell phone beeped, vibrated, or the smallest hint of light would shine through it, I would be up and alert. He never moved, and I sneaked a glance at my cell phone to find out the time. It was 1:26 AM. I sprung up, like the exorcist sitting straight up in the bed.

"Hey. Hey, your cell phone is ringing. Someone just called you." I nudged his arm.

"Ok, well I'm sleep. I will get it in the morning."

"Basketball season is over. Kobe didn't score any points today. There were no major trades. You can't tell me that one of your boys is calling you after 1 o'clock. You need to find out who called you. It could be an emergency, and I want to know who called you because it could be some girl."

His eyes rolled. I didn't give a damn how he felt. There had been times before when I pretended to not be bothered by late phone calls, but now it was time to call him out. He dragged his left arm towards his cell phone, and he checked the number.

"It is a girl Jazzmine. She is just a friend, and it's not even like that. Trust me. "

"Who is this friend, and why the hell isn't she sleep?"

"You heard me talk about her before. We dated while I was in college. She had kidney issues and almost died, and we remained friends. Just friends."

"No, that's the girl that you told me that you were fucking when we broke up just after I gave birth to our son."

"Look. It is not like that between us anymore. She has health issues Jazzmine, and sometimes she does not have anyone to turn to. You know that I am a loyal guy. I hate to turn my back on people."

"You need to call that bitch, and tell her not to call you anymore. I don't care if she has health problems you ain't no damn doctor."

"There is no need for that. We are just friends. I don't have to call her and tell her not to call. You are worrying about nothing, and that is not necessary." I played the tell-her- not-to-call card, and he handed me the we-are-just-friends card. I decided to drop the subject and went to sleep.

The following Monday I called in sick for work. I had two missions. One was to make some male friends that could always call my phone at any hour of the night and to check out the KIPP charter program for the new school year. Both missions were complete by the end of the business day.

Twenty Feet Tall

SUMMER SAID ITS final goodbye, and I carried my relationship with Ryan through the oil stained snow like a dead arm all winter long. We staged a few date nights in order to reclaim our relationship. They eventually became a casting couch for who could pitch the best moments of our son's life. Our daily conversations were bombarded with who owed him money, the laziness of his employees, the housing market crash, and whatever negative news that seemed to fly into Ryan's crosshairs. Finally, I just asked him, "Are you always so negative?"

His response was, "That is just my personality."

In all of these years, how did I not pick up on that? To deal with a round the clock Debbie Downer was emotionally draining.

Over the summer, I planned a trip that he had to cancel due to his work load. The kids and I went anyway and Lisa, my second mom, and my little brother tagged along. We had a great time without Ryan.

Lisa asked me during that trip, "Do you really want to go through a marriage with Ryan." I said, "Yes of course."

"It's not going to be fun. It will be a dull and boring marriage. So, why do it when you can take care of yourself and your children? When was the last time you and Ryan had fun together?"

I needed a microscope to scan my brain for a moment that would impress her. "We cook together, and we do things with the kids." Lisa poured me a strong drink after I made that statement.

"Marriage is about stability and security. It isn't called a circus. It is called a marriage."

I was trying to convince Lisa and myself that walking away from my relationship with Ryan solely based on the fact that it was not fun was irresponsible, and I left it at that. And now this winter, I had to do something else to help me hold on a little longer. Not to the idea of marrying Ryan, I had sadly given up on it and no longer looked forward to it. I had two childhood dreams. One was to be married. The other was to have larger breasts. Since Ryan and I were not getting married anytime soon, I could make one of my dreams come true all by myself.

I talked to Morgan about her "job" and my aunt Lynn about her "job," and they encouraged me to go for it. I went to a local surgeon by the name of Dr. Macklin, and he was cute enough to just visit without an exam. His nurse took pictures of my A-cups and Dr. Macklin came into the exam room.

"Jazzmine, I understand that you would like the implants. I want to inform you up front that in 20 years, you will have to have the implants replaced. You have small breast, but the tissue is very firm. You really don't need the surgery."

"Dr. Macklin, does anyone really neeeed the surgery?" I asked sarcastically.

"This is how I determine the right size implants. Choose a number.

1. People will barely notice your implants, but you will look better without a top on.
2. You will look great in a t-shirt, and men will still be able to look you in the eye.
3. Everyone will notice you, and men will hold every conversation with you staring at your cleavage. Which will it be?"

"I will take a 2.5." I scheduled the appointment without consulting my pseudo-husband and went on my merry way.

Ryan was pissed about the entire process.

"You didn't ask me how I felt about you getting a boob job. You told me. Those breasts were not for me. I am an ass man. I don't care about breasts."

"I did it for myself." This response made him extremely suspicious. And the nerve of him to think that every major move that I made had to include him, when he had not made any major moves on my behalf, but he had a major move coming.

His beautiful home that he had purchased was severely upside down. He finagled a way to short sell his house. His original plans were to rent an apartment or a house. Not once did he hear me say, "Come live with me in my condo." In our past, I had brought this up and asked him to move in with me so that we could save money. That was when I was intoxicated with love and delusional. Now, I thought that our living arrangements were just fine.

He started coming over my house every night. The first week or so I saw apartment books, but after that, he brought in more and more clothes. Six weeks went by, and I said to myself, "Oh shit, we live together."

My titties were healing up. I had a few girl trips on the books, and I didn't have "playing house" on my calendar. I wasn't feeling this scenario at all. I had a mental escape route planned. Ryan had shown me time and time again the type of husband that he would be. If I married him, I would have to settle for a little bit of attention from him and a little bit of cheating. Ryan will always be an exceptional dad, and if I ever needed anything, he would be more than willing to lend me a hand, so why should I buy the cow when I can get the milk for free?

A Women's Got to Have I

I KNOW WHY the caged bird sings. It's the same reason why broken hearted women love. It's in our nature. When love splashes, it adds color to this black and white world. Love supersedes wisdom and credits virtuous idealism. Man can develop a set of laws and religious ways to live by, but we only have a veneer of a great society when love is not resting peacefully inside the walls. When love does not sit at the table the acidic hearts of men can melt every structure and convention and reduce it all to dogma. I love to love, and I do it even when it's not reciprocated.

My work day ended early and I was home by 3:00 pm. While Cody played with his cars, I seasoned some chicken wings to put in the oven. I had evolved past the point of frying chicken. Frying required too much time and attention, but I still loved fried chicken. To give my chicken some sort of crisp, I drizzled a little vegetable oil on it before I put it in the oven.

"Mommy, mommy, mommy." I wasn't sure how long Cody had been trying to get my attention. I stopped cooking to give him my full undivided attention.

"Calisa told me wast to do." At three years old, Cody could express himself completely, and I paraphrased his statement to mean that the little cute girl with curly hair and rosy cheeks was bossing Cody around.

"What did you do after Calisa told you wast to do?"

"I told her wast to do back."

"You didn't like it when Calisa told you wast to do?"

"No, mommy I want you to tell Calisa wast to do." Three year olds are so cute at this age. I knew that this situation didn't need any parental intervention, but I wanted him to know that I was on his side.

"Does Miss Jennifer tell you wast to do?"

"Ju Ju is posed to tell me wast to do." At three he knew that he was supposed to respect authority. Our household was not set-up the way that I had imagined it, but my kids were of sound mind and spirit.

I was so disappointed that the summertime didn't set a stage for a barbecue with all of my friends and family followed by a much anticipated proposal. November came and went and there was no birthday proposal either. Just another gift that was a check off the box for Ryan. The Christmas holiday season was in full swing, and I really wanted Ryan to get the gift right this time. It was already bad enough that he didn't propose. He should really be giving me some luxurious gifts to buy more time and try and work himself out of the red. Ryan's emotional bank with me was well overdrawn.

My friends knew that Ryan was a horrible gift giver, and they even called him around the holiday to give him a few clues. I decided to lead by example this year and show him an example of an appropriate gift.

Toni and Erin waited in Erin's living room waiting for me to show up, so that we could all ride together and buy gifts for our significant others. When I arrived, they were discussing the perfect mall route.

"See Toni if we go to West County Mall first, we can knock out the small items on our Christmas lists at the same time." Erin slid on a pair of Ugg boots to compliment her leggings and puffy coat.

"I want to go to Frontenac first, so I can price this purse that my girl has been hinting at." Toni looked at the internet on his phone and pulled up several images of Gucci bags for the woman that finally put an end to his player ways.

"Whatever, it doesn't matter to me. I'm good either way." It didn't matter to me where I went. I was more concerned with where Ryan would go for me. Frontenac won over West County. Erin found a simple yet distinguished looking Burberry shirt and a bottle of cologne for her guy. Toni purchased a Gucci bag for his lady to add to the other smaller gifts that he had purchased. I couldn't find a damn thing.

"Let's just go ya'll. I will get Ryan's gift later."

"You may as well get in now girl. When will you have time to shop? Just get it and get it over with. If you find something else at a different store then you can return it." Erin tried to keep me focused on the task at hand.

"Look. He's a man, and take it from me, he doesn't care what you give him." Toni was simple in taste, and Ryan was a pretty low key guy. He liked to buy himself nice things but he didn't care to receive expensive gifts.

"I know most men don't trip off of gifts, but this is more for me to show Ryan how I would like to be treated."

"Get him the khaki colored casual Prada shoes that we saw in Saks."

"OK Erin, I don't want to get him Prada, and he shows up with some crap for me."

"He won't. I will give him a call and give him a hint."

I purchased the Prada shoes, and the kids picked out gifts, so that he could unwrap gifts from them as well. Cody chose a kid like neck tie, and Cassidy struggled harder than I did to choose something and eventually settled on a pack of dress socks. Erin reached out to Ryan but the conversations were too brief to insert the hint.

Santa came on Christmas morning. Ryan made biscuits, eggs, and bacon before the kids realized it was Christmas morning. When the aroma and daylight hit them, they both came down the steps. Underneath the tree was everything they had asked for and everything I thought that they should have. Ryan went to his car to get my gift.

"Merry Christmas Jazzmine." I took a deep breath and eyed the two wrapped gifts cautiously. I opened the first gift. It was a pink, fluffy mom robe. "This is from the kids." *Whew, he almost scared me.*

"Thanks babies." I kissed Cassidy and Cody on their cheeks.

"This is from me."

It was a small box, and all of my neurons started jumping. I opened the box and my daughter looked over my shoulder eagerly anticipating the discovery of my new treasure.

"Thanks." I eyed the watch and tried my very best to find something about the watch that I liked. The black leather band was thin with white stitching. The face of the watch was square and bedazzled with small crystals. Ryan had found the perfect clearance watch for someone's great aunt in a nursing home. For me, this watch did more than tell the time.

He opened the gifts that I purchased for him, and he was relieved as he opened the package with the tie and happy to receive socks and embarrassed by the shoes.

Erin hosted Christmas day at her home annually, and we joined her family. This year she chose a seafood theme. She could not wait to get me into her bedroom so that I could tell her what Ryan had bought me for Christmas. Toni was in the living room, and he was anxious to find out as well.

"So girl, how did he do?" In silence I lifted up my hand to sport my watch.

"Damn J, I'm sorry."

"Who would you buy this watch for Erin?

"Ugh, not my Mom, not my aunt, maybe...a teacher. No, I wouldn't give it as a teacher gift. I would just give it away to anybody."

"I am so pissed, but I am not going to let this ruin my Christmas. I'm going to need you to pour me an extra strong drink."

"Yeah, I will do that for you. It's the thought that counts J."

"If this is what his thoughts came up with then I don't need that mothafucka thinking about me." We laughed our way out of her bedroom. I hung around for about an hour. I didn't want to stay long and after a few hands of spades, I announced that we were leaving. Ryan had to use the restroom and Erin yelled to me in front of Toni, "Show him your watch." I lifted my arm exposing the worse gift of the year.

"That nigga don't give a fuck. Whatever he does to you at night I need to watch." I showed him a perfectly erect middle finger.

"What did he think about the shoes?" Erin's voice was just above a whisper.

"He liked them of course but he had a dumb look on his face." Ryan came out of the restroom, and we ended the conversation.

"Jazzmine, you're leaving us, huh?" Toni said.

"Yes, me, and the fam are up."

"What time is?" Toni's question was loaded with sarcasm and humor, and Ryan put Cody's coat on. Cody's energetic body was completely unaware of the comedy hour. Cassidy walked out of the room with her eyes peeled to her new Kindle that her father bought for her, unaware of anyone in the building.

"Time for me to leave, Toni." I walked out of Erin's Christmas party struggling to love.

Ryan never went all out for holidays, and it would be more acceptable if we were married. At least I would have a ring to sport, but this ain't right. It ain't right in the eyes of the street or the Lord. I need to tell him not to worry about giving me the perfect ring to commemorate the beginning of our lives together as husband and wife. I should tell him to find me a short end of a stick.

Reciprocity

THE END OF the summer was marked by the day that my daughter returned from her dad's in Nashville. I couldn't wait for her to
return. I just hoped that she would leave her sassy mouth in Nashville.
Cassidy did not take well to Ryan moving in with us. She hated it for
several reasons. One reason being that she really wanted him to propose to me. Also, she slightly resented the relationship that Ryan
and Cody shared. We had girl talk sessions from time to time, and
she straight up told me that she thought that Ryan was only in our
house to be with Cody. Maybe she overheard a phone conversation
that I was having with my mom. I thought that was relatively harsh
for a 13-year-old to think and say. The school year started without
incident, and Ryan and Cassidy seemed to be at least tolerant of each
other. Ryan stayed clear of Cassidy and Cassidy snapped at him every
time she thought he might instruct her to do anything chore related.
One evening Cassidy and I drove to Target, and she started an out of
the blue conversation.

"Mom. Do you ever check Ryan's phone."

"No." I lied. The true answer was that I had not checked it within
the past year. Only because I didn't have enough interest in what I
would find.

"Cassidy, why would you even ask me a question like that?"

"No reason. I just asked."

As we shopped in the aisles of Target, I brainstormed all of the reasons that would prompt my child to ask such an outlandish question. After shopping, I decided to revisit the conversation.

"OK Cassidy, why did you ask me if I looked in Ryan's phone?"

"Nothing." The response did not make sense but at the end of this conversation, I was determined to make a few things clear.

"Nothing what Cassidy. Go ahead spit it out."

"While I was on Ryan's phone playing a game, I started looking through his pictures and his messages. He had stuff on it from women, and I wanted to know if you knew?"

"Why would you look through his phone?"

"Mommy, he hasn't given you a ring, and when men don't commit it's probably because of another woman, and I wanted to know." Damn she had more common sense then I did. I refused to grant this conversation with any expression of emotion and remained very Hillary Clintonish during the entire car ride until I searched for the appropriate response.

"I understand that you love your mother, and you are concerned, but Cassidy, you don't have to worry about utilities in the house, a roof over your head, or food on the table, and I don't want you to concern yourself with Mommy's relationship. Do you understand?"

"Yes Ma'am."

"And always be respectful of the privacy of an adult. Don't go through his phone again do you understand?"

"Understood."

I maintained my Clintonish profile and didn't make mention of the conversation with Ryan that evening. Every night no matter the problem or situation Ryan and I wrestled for a few minutes under the covers. I reached an orgasm despite our relationship problems because I had perfected the art of imagining that I am with someone else. That someone else was not a movie star or an ex-boyfriend. It was the man that Ryan used to be towards me and how he used to make me feel. He was a little cocky and full of himself, but he was confident, relaxed, upbeat and very much into Jazzmine.

Set it Off

PSEUDO-MARRIED LIFE HAD its advantages. Our daily routine was more efficient. Ryan cooked, helped with household chores, and helped Cassidy with her homework. We loved our family and each other. Our real marriage might work out after all, but my circus fun would probably only happen with my family and friends. The final event of the fall was not the apple pie recipe that Ryan and I perfected, it was TSU's homecoming, and my crew was ready.

My entire crew met at Erin's house. The original time of departure was 11 am. Luckily neither Erin, the makeup guru, or I was responsible for a time sensitive mission because we all traded places with being the latest to arrive. We finally left around 2 pm and Erin's mom came by the house to see us off.

"I remember when you girls first left to go away to TSU, and look at you now. I am so proud of you girls. You turned out to be such beautiful women." Her face captured the true pride of a mother's heart. To think we had trained for this occasion by building up our alcohol tolerance, I was almost ashamed.

We made it to Nashville safely and without speeding tickets. Chris called me several times while I was on the road to speak with Cassidy and to make sure that I was alert on the road. Chris and our relationship as parents and friends had matured by leaps and bounds since the infamous tampon protest. He was not perfect, but he did not give up, and I respected him for it. I didn't always get the check in the mail, but Cassidy did get free phone calls, and she had spent holidays with her father consistently. It was progress, and I prayed that their relationship would continue to blossom. Chris had a rough parenting patch for a few years in Cassidy's life but she would need the love from her dad for many more decades. He still had time to catch up in my mind.

When Chris picked up Cassidy, he left me an herbal peace offering for me and my girls, and I added it to our stash of alcohol.

"We don't want to get to these parties late. We should all get dressed and keep it moving." Maranda was afraid that if we stayed in our hotel rooms too long we would lose the intensity to go out and have a good time.

One by one, we took our turns in the bathroom, and surprisingly, we were all dressed and ready to go in less than two hours. This was a true testimony as to how well we traveled together as a group. We pre-gamed with solo cup cocktails.

In the parking lot we set a match to the herbal offering and began to pass it around. We complimented the smooth ride from St. Louis to Nashville with a few random conversations about old flames in college. I honestly did not have any old flames that I anticipated running into. In life, I hadn't really been a flinger. Most of my sexual occurrences took place while I was in a relationship. I had a two-year jump off in college, but he lived in London. I knew that my friends and I would party like we did not have a care in the world, and I was totally OK with the weekend being void of a "happy ending."

The car stayed firm in its resting position but all of the passengers ascended into a higher realm. We were just about ready to go into the club when an Aston Martin pulled up right in front of us.

"OKKK." My homegirl with a blonde pixie cut raised her eyebrows.

"Wait ya'll don't get out the car let's be noisy." The makeup specialist freshened up her makeup, and we all followed suit.

"They some cuties." Aisha passed around a pack of gum.

"Yes, they are, and the driver purchased that car to make sure all the lil girls knew that he was different from the rest of the lil boys. Imma tell him to call me." I looked at my nails and pulled potato chip dust from in between them.

"J, you silly. We need to watch you and learn." My girl was just as enamored by my ability to attract people as I was enamored by her ability to maintain order in her life. We all needed to watch each other and learn.

The scene in the club was everything we prepared for it to be and more. We dropped it like it was hot; picked it up and dropped it again. I spotted an old collegiate friend that I had flirted with on a mental and physical level for years. We were never intimate but we were close in a way that we could never figure out.

The DJ played cadences from the Aristocrat of Bands, TSU's marching band and the party turned mad. These were tunes and beats that were the heartstrings of every TSU student and alumni. Somewhere in that space, I exchanged phone information with one of the gentlemen that we spotted in the parking lot. I wasn't sure if he was the driver or passenger, and it was of no concern to me. My flirtatious spirit was fed by focusing, aiming, and shooting my target out of the sky. My belly was full enough, and I never ate my kill. It was all for sport, and I did not even register his name into my brain.

On the way to the hotel, I never mentioned the guy that I met. My crew was drained and we were all asleep within 10 minutes after we put on our pajamas. That night we recharged and prepared ourselves for another epic moment, the pep rally.

We fell short on our targeted departure time of arrive at the pep rally. When we arrived at Gentry Stadium, we joined close to 11,000 of our fellow alums and current students. In the center of the stadium were the budding sprouts of the Divine Nine. The ladies of Delta Sigma Theta Sorority, Inc., Alpha Chi chapter, lined up for-tuitously. The men of Omega Psi Phi Fraternity, Inc. hopped in their shiny gold boots and army fatigue pants.   The men of Alpha Phi Alpha Fraternity, Inc. hissed and moved in a snake like rhythm. The ladies of Alpha Kappa Alpha Sorority, Inc. acknowledged their beauty in the palms of their hands. A chain of 45 brothers from Kappa Alpha Psi Fraternity, Inc. shimmied to a beat and smoothed out the wrinkles in their shirt in between steps. A blue wave of men and women streamed through the crowd representing the women and men of Phi beta Sigma Fraternity, Inc. and Zeta Phi Beta Sorority, Inc. The dainty ladies of Sigma Gamma Rho Sorority, Inc. let it be known that they were small in numbers but in the building while the men of Iota Phi Theta Fraternity, Inc. held up their shields. The nucleus of all historically black colleges lies within the power of the Divine Nine. It is where women and men pledge to live a life that benefits the greater good of all mankind.

My decision to join a sorority came as a shocker to most people who really knew me. I was such an individual in my own right, but I wanted to broaden my character and connect with causes that were bigger than me and that is how my initial curiosities were formed. Initially, I was interested in being an AKA. I learned the history of the organization, and I wanted to know more. Somehow I asked enough questions to be put in contact with a member on campus. I don't remember her name, but she had warm brown skin and dreadlocks like me. She was known for writing poetry and her academic achievements. Eventually, we had a conversation about the sorority.

The conversation was a disaster. She asked me what were "Excuses" and she was not impressed with my answer. I knew the gist of the riddle, but I didn't think she had earned the right to ask me such a question. At the time, I was washing up my daughter in a dorm room sink. In between classes, I volunteered at McKissick Middle School and answered letters from incarcerated women who had written grievances to the local chapter of the NAACP all while maintaining my position on the Dean's List. I didn't really know in my heart what excuses were, and I never learned.

I became disinterested in joining a sorority after that conversation. Something so superficial was not worth my time. Then, I had a change of heart, after my best friend Erin became a member of Delta Sigma Theta Sorority, Inc. She had described it as a life changing bonding experience. I started researching the history of Delta Sigma Theta Sorority, Inc. I fell in love with the statue of Fortitude, and it described the friendship bond that I shared with Erin to the letter. In college we were roommates in Wilma Rudolph Hall. In one room, with one light and a small bathroom with only a shower we lived together with my one-year-old daughter, Cassidy. Whatever sisterhood she was a part of was worth my time and sweat.

This may be a blasphemous explanation to legacy southern women who are born bred and groomed into Greek life, but I was from St. Louis, and in the Lou, it's a better explanation than most. And in Delta there are no perfect Deltas only active and inactive Deltas. Similar to organized religion, organized sisterhood is a lifetime commitment and struggle, but to thee I pledge.

The pep rally trumped the party from the night before, and my crew was ready to keep the party going. Next stop...the tea party, which never served tea. We all piled up in the car and made our ways to the next event.

As I walked up the elevator I spotted the guy from the night before, "Shit what is his name?" He looked cuter than he did the night before. I should have at least remembered the man's name. I smiled his way and moved into the crowd with my girls.

On our way out, our paths crossed once again.

"Hey what ya'll getting into later?" He had an educated southerner accent, my favorite.

"I'm not really sure. Text me, and I'll let you know." I had exchanged numbers with a few sorority sisters that I wanted to reconnect with, and I didn't remember his name. So I asked.

"What did you say your name was again?"

"It's Preston. That's the third time you asked me that like I'm some kind of lame."

"It's been a long night. Don't mind me."

"Are you on Facebook?"

"Yes." I gave him my Facebook name and accepted his friend request. Well I know I won't forget his name now. Thanks Facebook. Innocently, I walked through the crowd and disappeared into the next wave of fun.

TSU's centennial weekend was everything that we had dreamed and prepared for it to be. The makeup specialist gave me the name "Ball Buster" for tenaciously flirting and dry humping people without finishing them off. A small match began to burn in Erin's heart for a special someone. My conservative girlfriend kept us all in line and made sure we didn't get too crazy. As for the rest of us, we all pushed it as far as we could go.

Don't Play That Song

MY ACTION PACKED summer along with the centennial home-coming celebration drained my energy reserves and slowed my little tail to a very slow wag. Ryan never said anything, but I knew I was going out too much, overspending, and over travelling. I had certainly suffered from the Benjamin Button disease, and it was time for me to start acting like a grown up again.

The unseasonably warm late October grazed the faces of Cody and Cassidy as we walked to Cassidy's bus stop. Along the way, Cassidy told us about her weekend with her dad in Nashville. He taught her how to play a card game, and they went shopping. I even called him occasionally to vent and get parenting advice. My heart glowed at the strides that her father had made. We came along way...baby.

Cody tried his best to force the details of his weekend into the conversation. The only point that Cassidy and I acknowledged was that he had went to Kansas City with Ryan, and they had dinner at a dinosaur restaurant. The bus stop conversation belonged to Cassidy. I planned to catch up with Cody during the ride to daycare.

At four years old, Cody was already a master conversationalist. He loved to talk. He made sure that his listeners were engaged, and he asked questions regularly to make sure that you were tuned in.

On the way to daycare, he couldn't wait to talk about his weekend in Kansas City, and he finally had my undivided attention.

"Mommy, I ate at a restaurant with dinosaurs."

"Wow, did you eat a dinosaur?"

"No, they were not real mommy. They were fake, and they couldn't bite us."

"Did you eat your food at the dinosaur restaurant?" Cody was a horrible eater, and he enjoyed going to restaurants more than eating at them.

"Yes, I ate all of my food, and my girlfriend Candice ate all of her food, too."

"Your girlfriend went to Kansas City with you?"

"She lives in Kansas City at my uncle Kenny's other house."

"Is your girlfriend big like mommy or little like you?"

"She's big like you mommy." Oh shit. I remembered the name Candice. When I asked Ryan about the name he shrugged and said she was JP's adoptive daughter. Ryan is either a philanthropist with a mission to expose adopted children to short distance travel or a lying son-of- a-bitch.

"What did your Uncle Kenny have for dinner at the restaurant?"

"My Uncle Kenny was not there." Cody stared out the window in search of something more interesting to focus on.

"What did your daddy eat?"

"He ate chicken bones with Candice."

"What did you do after dinner? Did you go to the movies?" I used a kindergarten teacher's tone so that I could get the juice out of every detail as I prepared a case to present to Ryan after work.

"No, we got ice cream."

"Did you get into the car to get ice cream?"

"Yes, we went in Candice's car."

"Wow, buddy. Your girlfriend can drive. I'm impressed. She may be too big for you."

"No she's not. I am getting bigger and bigger, and tomorrow I will be big like daddy."

"What kind of ice cream did you get?"

"Uhmm, chocolate. No, strawberry."

"What kind did your girlfriend have?"

"Chocolate."

"Did your dad have any ice cream?"

"No."

"What kind of ice cream did your Uncle Kenny have?"

"My Uncle Kenny was not there!" His voice was raspy and annoyed by the fact that I ignored him the first time that he mentioned his Uncle Kenny's absence.

"Were you sleepy after your ice cream?"

"Yes, and we went to my Uncle Kenny's other house."

"Where did you sleep?"

"With my dad and my girlfriend."

"Where did your Uncle Kenny sleep?"

"Mommy! I told you my Uncle Kenny was not there." He slapped his forehead in disgust and I held the plug that sealed my true emotions.

I dropped Cody off at daycare, kissed him on the cheek and filed our conversation in the bullshit that I will deal with after work folder.

My journey to Southern Illinois and the news surrounding the upcoming presidential elections helped to redirect my focus. I switched stations between liberal and conservative perspectives. When both sides became too depressing, I tuned in to Howard Stern. Each channel provided an escape from my reality. Perhaps an escape from reality is the origin of political interest for everyone. It sure was for me.

I made it to the Howard Stern Chanel quicker than usual this morning. Howard was expressing his opinion of Tod Akin and his legitimate rape phrase. I had to call Collin, my business partner. He was the only person that I knew that would enjoy this type of humor.

"What up?" Collin practiced using slang terms from the 90's with me. He knew that the phrases were dated, and they made him more of a funny guy than a cool one.

"Yo, did you hear Howard's comments about Senator Tod Akin?" I never said yo during a conversation, but I wanted to be funny too.

"No, I haven't listened all morning."

"Well, Robin cited the poll results for Senator Akin. His approval rating was neck and neck with McCaskill even though Akin made that stupid legitimate rape comment. Howard said that those statistics were proof that that people in Missouri were idiots and that America should give Missouri back to the Indians. That was funny as hell."

Colin laughed and we transitioned into a conversation that was taboo in the workplace, a political conversation: red versus blue, republicans versus democrats. We held these forums amongst ourselves regularly, and we did it without offending each other at the end of the work day. Our secret was a race relationship shift that is rarely spoken about. We shifted from a state of tolerance to love. I grew to love Collins family and he grew to love mine. And we both loved America. Love triumphs over politics every time, and it helps you understand an alternative perspective.

"Senator Akin is a pin head, and he fucked it up for us." Colin was a true believer of the Republican Party and took ownership of the party like it was his favorite sports team.

"I agree he was a shoe in. McCaskill was not even in the running."

"We could lose the Senate because of him. He should resign. I hate him. We could have gained control of the White House and the senate. I'm tired of funding the lifestyle of people who are too damn tired to wake up and go to work every morning."

"I see your point Collin, but what about the grocery store chains that have made millions from patrons spending food stamps or real estate moguls that have made fortunes from subsidized housing? These organizations work hard and are creating jobs from the support of people who do not wake up and go to work every morning.

These people are not the problem. They only re-shuffle our tax dollars, but they are the scapegoats."

"You watch too many of those damn liberal talk shows and read
to many liberal magazines."

"No Collin. This is my life."

"Let me ask you a question? Are you pro-choice?" The irony of a
man asking a single mother with two children, both out of wedlock,
her stance on life made my eyebrows raise.

"Collin, I'm a single mother with two children. Do I really have to
explain what life means to me?"

"OK but you are the exception."

"Not really. You just know me."

"You are the exception. The average single mother in the black
community does not have a father in their children's lives."

"That's not true. They don't have husbands in their lives, but the
fathers are usually around in some capacity." He thought about this
statement hard, and he was still unconvinced. I couldn't explain it
either. It doesn't make sense, but way too often the woman that is
worth carrying a black man's baby and the woman that is worth carrying a black man's last name are two different people.

Later that night I presented my case to Ryan. I knew that he
would twist the situation into a pretzel that only existed in our son's
vivid imagination. I let the jury rest and threw the bullshit out of the
J's court of law due to lack of sufficient evidence, but as we laid side
by side, I decided to give a closer examination of the bird that I shot
down from the sky during homecoming weekend.

Tit for Tat

I PULLED OUT my iPhone and went to my Facebook account. I was so rusty in the meeting- new-people department that I didn't realize the scope of accepting a new friend on Facebook. It's' like saying, "Hi, nice to meet you," and whipping out a complete photo album of all of your family and friends.

Clicking on Preston's page felt invasive. All of my Facebook friends were people that I knew and wanted to keep in contact with. They were not strangers that I wanted to get to know. I had never used Facebook to judge a person's characters. He had asked for my Facebook information first, so I am pretty sure he had already profiled me. I rarely posted pictures, but I allowed my friends to tag me in their pictures. Usually, I was tagged at a party or during happy hour. I am certain that Preston has me pegged as a party girl.

I clicked on his name and then to his photo albums. As far as I could recall, he was a handsome man, but my recollection could have been skewed by the drinking and smoking. Thank you, Mark Zuckerberg, for creating a medium more reliable than my hazy memory. My first search was the hotness test. I scanned his pictures from Mexico. "Ohhhh he was a cutie." My intoxicated self knew what fine looked like. Next, I looked at a few of his mobile uploads. By then, I started to feel like a stalker. Someone snapped a picture of Preston while he was hugging a cute little four-year-old boy. *Can you say mommy porn?* The more I clicked the more my interest grew. I stumbled on a picture of his mother. Preston's mother looked like a sweet and stern lady. She looked like she sipped tea and ate crumpets. No way in hell would she be accepting of her son dating a woman with two children. It would take more than a few German chocolate cakes to win her over.

Of all the pictures that I looked at, none of them were with a woman that could stand out as a love interest. Then, I reflected on my profile. Ryan was not on a single picture on my page. Before I went to bed, I looked over at Ryan. He was snoring lightly, and it was a sound that I had grown accustomed to. It was the sound of night. My final thought for the night was, "It is better to deal with the devil that you know than the devil that you don't."

The next morning, I sipped my morning cup of coffee and ironed my work clothes. I said a silent prayer and thanked God for simple things in my life and my abundant blessings. I begged him for the strength to continue to be a "good woman." I felt like my good woman days were numbered. Preston lived in Memphis. The potential for him to be a threat in my relationship was minimal, but he could be a great temporary escape.

On the front porch of Cody's daycare, I decided to ask him once again if he had slept in the bed with "his girlfriend" and his daddy, while he was in Kansas City. His response was, "My dad told me that it's not very nice to say that Candice sleeps with me." I could tell that he was confused by the conversation, and Ryan had attempted to do a little damage control. I spent the rest of the car ride justifying my next move. I looked at my bare left ring finger, and that was all of the justification that I deemed necessary.

It was just passed 10 in the morning, and I had already called on most of my customers for the morning. I sat in the parking lot of my final morning stop and looked over sales numbers and emails. Then the phone rang. It was a 901 number. It was him. I accepted the phone call with my index finger and a smile.

"Hello, this is Jazzmine." I used a formal greeting to mask my teenage giddiness.

"Hi beautiful, this Preston."

"Hey Preston. How are you?"

"I'm good. You probably don't remember me."

"I remember you. We met at the tea party."

"No, we met the night before. You must have me confused with someone else." I could hear his southern smile through the phone.

"Stop it! It was you, but we did see each other at the tea party." I was quickly losing ground on my case for legalization of herbal remedies.

"You looked like you were having a good time. So, I will let you get away with the mix up."

"I appreciate it. Do you go to TSU's homecoming every year?"

"No, my alma mater plays in a different conference, but this year we played your team. That's the only reason why I came. We let ya'll win the game cuz it was your homecoming game. We didn't want to rain on ya'lls parade."

"Preston, it takes talent to rain on our parade. Your team did not have enough talent on the field to bring the rain."

"That's funny. You are a beautiful girl. I know you keep up a lot of trouble in St. Louis."

"Not at all." I answered with confidence and watched another salesperson get out of the car. I didn't motion to move. I was enjoying my conversation.

"Where your boyfriend at?"

"I don't have one." I lied earnestly. "We recently broke up." I lied again for good measure.

"How recently? Two days ago?" He said sarcastically.

"Two months ago." I lied for the third time, but I was not quick enough on my feet to change the two so I went with two months. It's usually bad to start off lying to a person. These lies were special. They were lies that I had never told before. They were lies of endearment.

"How about you? Where is your girl?"

"I don't have one, and I don't believe in girlfriends. The only title I believe in is a wife." Somewhere in Memphis, an innocent girl is surely calling him her boyfriend. I would bet money on it.

"What do you do?" I could hear his smile through the phone again.

"I am a pharmaceutical sales representative. And yourself?"

"I'm retired." Boom. I summarized his work history in a blink of a second. This brother owns a barber shop, a carwash, and deals drugs. Within the next two years he will be indicted. And a voice in my head said, "Now Jazzmine, you need to get back to your devil at home?"

"You retired from what." My lips turned with my eyebrows.

"I taught school for a few years. Then, I started selling insurance. I established a large book of businesses through a few family networks. Last year, I sold my agency and invested in real estate." Hot damn this boy might have real W-2's I told the voice in my head. He is a real...tax...paying...citizen.

"How old are you?" I had to know the age of the retiree.

"I am 31."

"How do you stay busy? Now, that you are...retired."

"I volunteer, and I manage my properties."

"And for fun?"

"I like to travel."

"I have been sitting in this parking lot talking to you for 30 minutes. Let me get back to work, and I will call you later." The conversation ended and his accent lingered in my mind and faded in front of Dr. Santos's receptionist.

"You can go on back Jazzmine. Dr. Santos is finished with his morning patients." I walked into a well-organized office lined with books unrelated to medicine.

"Dr. Santos what's new? I reached for my sales aids and took a seat in front of his desk.

"I leave for the Philippines on Sunday."

"When will you be back?"

"I am staying until the new year."

"You will be gone for two months? Take me with you Doc." We both laughed. "How is Christmas in the Philippians?"

"It's amazing."

"Will you have a Christmas tree?"

"Yes but it will be different from an American tree."

"Does your family host a large celebration?"

"Yes we feed about one hundred people."

"Wow! It must take weeks to prepare food for one hundred people."

"We don't cook the dinner. The staff prepares the dinner for us." He didn't say this with arrogance. His tone was very a matter of fact and modest.

I like people of privilege that are modest. The money that they have in their bank accounts is usually the smallest issue that divides them from the rest of us. Moreover, it is the literature, music, wine, and food in their homes that separate the lifestyles.

Over the years of our blooming professional relationship, I learned that he loved classical music against his ears, wagyu beef tenderloin to chew and Malbec to wash it down. He read the most random non-fiction genres like books on locally grown produce and how to prepare it. One weekend, I downloaded the book that he was reading on locally grown produce. Picked up a few steaks and a bottle of Malbec and for around $10 a day, I imitated the ways of a general's son. Every time I visited his office, I could not wait to hear about his adventures, and he loved to hear me share stories about my children. He was amazed that I could work as a single mother. Dr. Santos was shocked that I could keep a smile on my face, and he assisted its glow by prescribing my products. And it worked for me.

Our meeting went well, and I was on to my next stop. After driving the interstate for 70 miles, passing large towns that were considered large towns only because they had a Subway sandwich shop, slowing down through townships tucked away in cornfields, I arrived at Dr.

Young's office. I loved visiting this office. The staff was so friendly.
There was a mother and daughter nurse team, and we talked liked
old friends or favorite cousins.

"Is Dr. Young available?"

"You know he does not see reps anymore, but I'm sure he will let
you go back to his office." The receptionist left her desk to make sure
it was OK, and a few minutes later, I was flagged to go back.

"How is your family?" I leaned on the counter and grabbed a chocolate kiss from a candy dish.

"Last week, we took the kids fishing. Look at our pictures. They
turned out so cute." I looked through the photos and her children
were cutie pies. "Don't look at my husband. He is working undercover,
and he had to grow facial hair. I hate it, but I love him." She shuffled
a few patient charts and entered information into the computer.

"Sarah, I am not looking at you husband's facial hair. You have a
very beautiful family."

She stopped working on the computer and shifted all of her
attention on me.

"Has your daughter earned her room back?" Sarah's mother
asked. My life as a parent was a series of adventurous episodes, and
she could not wait to hear my updates.

In my last episode with my daughter, I evicted her from her room.
In my eyes, it was a sanitation hazard. I gave her 10 days to rectify
the situation. After the 10 days expired, I put a notice on her door to
evacuate the premises. I issued her a blanket and a pillow and allowed
her to sleep in the den on the futon.

"Yes, I gave Cassidy her room back, but she did not deserve it. She
had adjusted to her new life in the den and started leaving her mess in
the den area. Right now, I am in prayer mode and God will eventually
give me an answer for my daughter's junky ways." They laughed and
Dr. Young walked out of an exam room, and we discussed my products.
The exchange took about five minutes, and I was able to convince him
to use my products exclusively. Not a bad day at the office.

As soon as I jumped into the car, I called Ryan. I ended the call before the second ring. I didn't want to talk. I only wanted my number to show up on his cell phone missed call log. I planned to tell Ryan later that evening that I tried to call him and could not reach him. I didn't want to hear his voice.

I called Preston shortly after I placed my call to Ryan and he answered.

"Hello beautiful." The greeting made me blush, and if I would have smiled harder lipstick would have touched my ears. "How was work?"

"It went well. I have a two-hour drive ahead of me, but it was worth it."

"So what do you like to do when you are not working?"

"I like to travel of course, but when I am at home, I like to hang out with my family and friends. I'm not really big on club scenes, but I like to go to happy hours. I have a daughter that just turned 14 and a four-year-old. They keep me pretty busy." I knew my last comment would throw him for a loop. I was vibrant, stylish, thin, and I did not fit the typical mold of a single mother of two, the ideal unmarried woman of two children.

"Oh, you have two kids? Wow, you really know how to keep yourself together." I heard the uneasiness in his voice and adjusted the spotlight to shine on him.

"Do you have children?"

"No, but I want kids. I actually want a large family about five kids."

"Five, wow." This number made me feel uneasy. I probably had too many kids for him, and he wanted too many for me.

"How will you travel with five kids?"

"I would definitely need a nanny. I already have a housekeeper and it's just me."

"Five kids. That's a lot of dropping off and picking up especially when they start playing sports."

"Yeah, my nanny would have to help out with that."

"I heard that!" I thought it was a delusional way to shuffle a family of five, but who was I to judge? Really, who was I to judge?

We talked routinely for a couple of weeks only during the day time in between my office visits. This worked perfectly for me. I couldn't talk on the phone during the evening anyhow. I did give Preston a few evening phone checks to see if he would answer.

I waited for Ryan to leave the house to go to the store. Then I called Preston to see if he would answer. He never answered the phone after 5. Perhaps he only recognizes the title of girlfriend after 5 pm.

I wished he was local, and we could meet for a drink or go to the movies. He couldn't come over my house or anything, but I'm sure I couldn't go over his house either. Our involvement consisted of simple phone calls until he opened a small door.

"Hey J, what's your favorite place to travel?'

"It depends. Vegas is great to party. I like to vacation anywhere coastal, and I love the mountains."

"We should meet up somewhere. We can do somewhere in Florida or the Carolinas." Preston rambled off several cities none were on our home turf.

"I have a business meeting coming up in Philadelphia. You should meet me there." My suggestion surprised my own self. "We can catch the train to New York and grab dinner in the city." This was a rather ambitious itinerary, but for a man who planned to have five children, a housekeeper and a nanny, I felt it was feasible.

I was not surprised that he said yes, and then the very next day he backed out.

"J, I'm sorry I had plans for that weekend."

"What do you have planned?" I was not disappointed yet. I had every intention to change his plans.

"My boys and I are going to watch my alma mater play."

"Preston, your boys can go without you. They are big boys, and they can have a good time without you?"

He responded in a soft apologetic whine.

"I can't cancel. I always give my boys so much lip for backing out of plans."

"If you cancel, they will know that it is for an extreme circumstance. Besides you already know your boys. You hang out with them all of the time. You have never hung out with me." I made this statement like it was all that he needed to hear to make a well informed decision.

"Let me think about it." The next day he sent a text message saying SEE YOU IN PHILLY.

With You

I LISTENED TO the flight attendants demonstration on how the passengers should conduct themselves in the event of an emergency. I heard this performance dozens of times, but it felt brand new and interesting. I even looked under my seat and took the time to figure out how it could be manipulated into a flotation device. Then, I thought that it would make more sense if it turned into a parachute. Odds are we would crash over land. What good would the flotation device do us? It didn't make sense. Just like the fact that I would be spending an entire weekend with a strange man did not make sense. Me and whomever developed the airplane seat cushions were not playing with a full deck.

For almost a year I lived in Philadelphia. Ryan made one visit to Philly to visit, and he helped me move back to St. Louis. I could never convince him to meet me in the cities that I visited for business. I once stayed at a really nice hotel in Coconut Grove near Miami. Ryan couldn't make it. I lived in Baltimore on the Harbor for an entire year, and Ryan never visited me there either. And I never invited anyone else, but I invited Preston like I was a pro.

He wasn't scheduled to arrive until the second day of my work convention, and part of me was excited and the other part of me wished that he wouldn't show up. On the first day of my work convention, I worked hard to impress potential customers and even harder to stuff my brain with thoughts that did not involve the strange man that I was going to spend the weekend with.

My work responsibilities lasted until noon. After work, I paced the center city of Philadelphia and shopped in a few boutiques. My journey ended at Rogue, a cute wine bar in Rittenhouse Square with a picturesque view of the park.

The moon shared the sky with a remnant of sunlight from the day. The trees strutted while standing in place, sporting all of the best shades of autumn. The temperature was 70 degrees in early November, and I felt partly responsible for the unseasonable heat. I was hot!

Minutes after my waitress brought out my glass of cabernet and an assortment of artisan cheeses, I was noticed by a handsome man that appeared to be leaving from work. He was the seventh man that day that made a b-line to come and speak to me and offer me his card. There must have been something on me.

That night I drifted to sleep peacefully after reading a novel, but that morning, I didn't wake up alone. I woke up with Aunt Flow which was fine by me. It gave me a guaranteed excuse for not having "relations" with the stranger.

I reported to the convention site at 8:15 am. I was scheduled to work until noon, and Preston's flight was schedule to land at 1:30. The sand from my hour glass poured rapidly, and before I knew it, my shift was over. I swallowed the lump in my throat and struggled to cling to the vixen that had apparently invited a stranger to this business trip.

The water from my 10 minute shower washed the vixen away, and I started to panic. In the midst of my attack, my cell phone rang.

"Hey, I just touched down." I used my remaining nerves to ask him about his flight and give him the address to the hotel. After the call ended, I knew that he would be standing in my room in less than 20 minutes. I slipped on a pair of jeans and a black t-shirt, strategically put on my make-up and placed an emergency call to my BFF.

"Erin. What...in...the...fuck...am...I...doing?"

"Calm down bestie. You are having fun. Is he there yet?"

"No, he is on his way." I curled up into a ball on the edge of the bed. My eyes were bucked and shifty like in horror movies.

"Have fun." She said in an ooh-la-la kind of way.

"This man is going to think I'm a hoe."

"So what? He is only one person on the planet. If he is the only person in the world that thinks you are a whore. You will be fine."

"Erin that shit that you just said is not good advice, and I started my period so I can't be a whore even if I wanted to."

"Well, there you go. No booty for him."

"We are traveling to New York and having dinner at Mr. Chow. He has some kind of sexual expectation. I'm sure."

"Since when did you start sleeping with men for Chinese food?" I needed that joke, and I started to create a scheme for avoiding any potential sexual acts.

We would go to dinner. After dinner we would go to the club. I would have a little to drink and make sure he had a lot. We would then go to a strip club. There, I would spot a big booty girl and buy him a lap dance and even more drinks. Finally, we would return to the room and according to my plan he would pass out. I intended on repeating this plan the following night.

Forty minutes passed while I ran my mouth with Erin on my personal cell phone. I didn't realize that the battery had shut down on my work phone and Preston only had that cell number. I charged my work phone, and I read three text messages from Preston. He had been in the lobby for almost 30 minutes. I called him immediately.

"Hellooo." He answered the phone as if he was opening a door to an abandoned building.

"Preston, I didn't realize my phone was off."

"I'm hundreds of miles from home, and you had me stranded in the lobby for 20 minutes." It was more like 30 but who was counting?

"Sorry, the room number is 403 come on up."

"Ok, I'm walking to you now. You probably don't even remember what I look like."

"Yes I do. You were about my complexion, and you were wearing a green shirt when I met you."

"No, my shirt was white." I laughed hard and thought of a comeback.

"The light from the club made it look green."

"I am about five foot three inches, and I was wearing glasses."

"You are not five foot three and you were not wearing glasses."

"How would you know?"

"Hey, if you think that I don't know what you look like, and you took two planes to come and visit me, then you must think that I look like Beyoncé. He laughed, and we lost our connection as he got into the elevator.

The knock on the door was my cue to live in the moment. I opened the door with a childlike grin. He carried his duffle bag into the room and shook his head and pointed to his watch. He plopped on the queen size bed that had not been touched. I hoped he was comfortable because that was the bed that I assumed that he would sleep in.

I eye scanned his body from toe to head and then from head to toe.   I took in all of his facial features one at a time. His eyes were small and bright. His nose was broad and masculine. And his lips… And his lips were soft, plump and perfectly defined. I pushed my lips to the side and spoke.

"This weekend will be a character stretch for me."

"We will see." I didn't know what to make of his response. I was in the business of building relationships, and I could entertain a frog, snake, or a lion.

"So do you have any brothers or sisters?" I bit my lip. I deserved an ass whooping from my father for this.

"I have a sister and a brother." All I knew about Preston, I learned from Facebook. We hadn't really talked much about anything personal.

I knew that people were crazy in this world, and if at the end of all of this, I was still alive, then it would count as a good time.

I made small talk about my family and away we went. We walked from the hotel to the Continental Diner. Our personalities were instant matches, and I congratulated my under the influence self for having such good taste in men. I couldn't have imagined a better candidate to cheat with.

"How much longer do we have to walk? We don't walk in Memphis."

"It's a nice day, and your legs will make it." Our conversation had been a series of basic questions and answers that one usually knows before you spend the night with a person. He carried the conversation, and I allowed him to. Then, I decided to switch the gears of the conversation.

"So, have you ever been in love?" I wanted to know how he registered on the fantasy scale.

"No, I love people, but I don't think I have ever been in love. If you define love by meaning that I care about someone's well-being. Then by that definition, I love you." Well, I'll be damned. I am walking down the yellow brick road with the tin man himself. I don't think Preston has a heart. I made a mental note to Google the nearest strip clubs while we were at the restaurant.

"Have you ever had unconditional feelings for a woman?"

"All feelings are conditional." He went into a rant that had something to do with cause and effect. Everything he said seemed rehearsed and well thought out. All he needed was a projector, a screen, and a slide deck on his philosophy of love, and he could put his show on the road.

"Do you have unconditional feelings for your mother?" This question caught him off guard, and I asked him a series of other questions. He started rambling. Then, he started stuttering. I stopped him in mid stutter and said, "You like the way I put that on you didn't ya?" My eyes met his eyes firmly, and he warned me, "Don't do that."

"That" had nothing to do with the conversation, but it was the seductive thing that I knew that I did.

"So, how do you define love Jazzmine?"

"Love is a feeling that you share with your family and friends and people that you can relate to."

"Can you relate to me?" I knew where he was headed with this question, and I tried to ease out of it. He asked me one question after the other until I began to ramble and stutter. He stopped me in mid stutter. Looked me into my eyes and said, "You like how I put that back on you don't ya?" No he did not just pull a me on me.

At that moment I decided to act like a lady and think like a girl for the next 48 hours of my life.

"My feet are starting to burn."

"Stop complaining. We almost there."

"You said that two blocks ago." We went back and forth like a seasoned couple. I felt way too comfortable around him which made me wonder. If he could make women feel so comfortable, why was he "single." So I asked.

"How long was your longest relationship?"

"Three months."

"What does a woman do to make you decide the relationship is over after only three months?"

"She doesn't do anything. It's mostly me. I have never had a woman to make me feel the way that she feels about me." I took that answer for the absolute truth not a personal challenge. Our weekend together was a standard length of a relationship for him, but it didn't matter. I had whole man at home. I kept smiling and walking.

We chose to sit at the bar and have dinner. The bartender was beautiful. She wore her hair natural, and it was cut in a bob. Her outfit was trendy, and it matched her bubbly personality.

"What can I get for you two?"

"I'll have a peach bellini." I looked over at Preston.

"Let me have 1800 and cranberry juice." You could usually tell a lot about a man based on his drink order, but this had me confused.

"You guys make such a cute couple. How long have you been together?"

"This is our first date." I replied with the best answer I could think of. It really was not a date. I ran away from home and met up with a stranger. Dates lead to relationships. This could lead me into a trash can in the alley.

I sat in the passenger side of the conversation wagon. We covered topics from family, sex, religion, and politics. There is a true art to having a conversation without revealing anything about yourself nor asking anything about the other person. In the ranks of this art, he was a mastermind. Our conversation was enriched with hypothetical situations, and it was entertaining.

"Let's roll; we are taking a cab back. I refuse to walk back."

"That's fine." We hailed a cab and jumped into the back seat. We went from 0 to 60 in less than 60 seconds. He leaned in to kiss me while pressing the back of my head closer to him. My hand touched the back of his head, and we gave each other one of those Evelynn Champagne, Kisses- Don't-Lie kisses.

We were only six blocks from the hotel, and by the time we made it to the hotel, I had touched everything on his body. According to Steve Harvey's book, women are supposed to wait 90 days before engaging in any sexual activity. In the heat of that moment, I wouldn't have even been able to count from one to 90. If it wasn't for Aunt Flow, the only thing that I could have done with a three-month calendar with this man was buy a box of crayons and color it.

We stumbled into the room kissing and touching. We played ratchet rap music and continued. In a very short time, I crossed Preston's neck line, lip line, and every other line, recklessly.

We fell asleep in a spooning position and I woke up to the sound of the cell phone duet. His cell phone went zzit zzit. My cell phone went buzz buzz, but we did not move our muscles.

My work day began and ended gracefully and by late afternoon we were headed to New York. We selected a seat in the front of the train in the handicapped section. There was enough room to fit my suitcase, and I propped my legs on top of it. I pulled out a splitter for my ear buds that would allow us to listen to music together. Preston selected Bobby Blue Bland from his playlist, I followed with Johnny Taylor and the battle of the blues ended with B.B King. We listened to old music as if we were old friends. Nothing seemed brand new about the time that went by. I was three years older than him, but our souls graduated from high school together in 1974.

A cycling taxi paddled us from Grand Central Station to our hotel. Time Square watched us as we passed through. A tourist from a double decker bus took a snapshot of us from afar. We were an attraction, and the tourist captured an unexposed image of black love. Thankfully, it was unexposed. The fully developed image would have a picture of Ryan and whoever the girl was calling Preston's cell phone last night. They would be trying to kill us both.

Mr. Chow was a great experience. I had been there several times before and every time I opened the door the decor was the same, but the experience was different. The white linens and modern decor enhanced both of our silhouettes. I looked Preston directly in the lips and waited for them to open.

"This is a really nice spot. Is the chef a world renowned chef?"

"Yes, and there is also a location in Beverly Hills. I don't really know the low down on the chef but the food is really good." Preston shifted in his seat and straightened his back.

"Have you ever wanted to open up a restaurant?"

"I have toyed with the idea but not really." Preston's eyes locked into mine.

"I'm thinking about opening a restaurant."

"On your own or with a group of investors?" My expression mirrored his and I became serious.

"On my own. There is really nothing in downtown Memphis catering to the young black professional crowd. My spot would be classy and fun."

"Make sure you find a good partner, or invest in a location that is already profitable. There are a lot of moving parts to a restaurant. It's a lot of work, and when you have all of those employees to manage in the front of the house and the back of the house, you will feel like you have more than five kids." He maintained his business posture and noted my feedback.

As we waited for dinner our conversation bounced and landed in natural rhythms. We talked about my career and my family.

"My grandfather owns land in Popular Bluff, MO. It is currently being rented out as farmland. The land is in a prime location. I really would like the land to stay in the family, and I was considering purchasing his share of the farm." I sipped my champagne cocktail and waited for him to respond.

"Do you know anything about farming?"

"No, the land is being rented out. I figured I would buy the land and become a farming expert later." Usually this approach worked.

"You should probably become an expert on farming first, before you spend your money. I don't mean to change your plans or critique your goals."

"No worries." I leaned back into my seat and finished off the rest of my drink. Maybe I shouldn't buy a farm. Hell, I can't even keep a cactus alive.

The waiter brought the food, and before Preston began to eat, he said a prayer over his food. I usually pray over my food, but this weekend was different, and I elected not to say any prayers because I didn't want God to know that I was there.

The food was amazing and I stared into the flame in front of me. Preston and I were mirrored images of each other. Complete diametric opposites. He plans shit. I just do the shit and hope it works for the best. He's a thinker I am a doer. He likes safety. I like adventure.

He loves with his mind. I love with my heart. Our interest and priori-
ties were almost identical. It was cute.

The next stop on the itinerary for the evening was the Underground
Lounge. We walked back to the hotel to change and listen to live
music. We walked into the hotel room and never made it out.

The night was a carbon copy of the night before until around 2
a.m. He went to the bathroom six times over a two hour stretch. I
figured that he was performing a damage control operation for the
home front or he was showing signs of type 2 diabetes. One or the
other.

Around 4 a.m. he showered and prepared to leave for the airport.
We said our goodbyes. The twinkle in his eyes stood still and flat, and
he shamelessly formed his lips into a partial smile. For the first time
all weekend he seemed distant and foreign.   He didn't say it, but I
heard, "*What are you looking at me for? I didn't come to stay.*"

"Take Care." He said with his plastered smile and gave me a hug
that he could have given to his kindergarten teacher.

"See you later." I headed back under the covers, and when I heard
the door shut, I smothered my face under the sheet hoping the angels
would not see me.

That's the Way Love Is

I CLOSED MY eyes and opened them a few hours after Preston left. I found a pair of yoga pants and a tank top to throw on. My shower was interrupted by my cell phone. I knew it was Ryan, and I would call him as soon as I stepped out of the shower. The phone rang again and again. When I looked at the missed call it was Preston, and I dialed his number.

"Hey J, I left some clothes behind. Could you look for my jeans and a button up shirt?"

"OK, let me check." I search on the side of the bed. "Yep you left them. Text me your address, and I will mail them to you." I put his clothes in a plastic bag and held the bag far away from me as if the articles were laced with radioactive cooties.

I had already created a script for Ryan detailing my weekend. Men's clothing was not a part of the story line.

My flight departed at noon. As soon as I arrived in St. Louis, I grabbed my luggage and headed directly to FedEx. I was on a mission to mail Preston his shit back. I picked up each item and placed it into the box and dropped the box on the counter like it was a giant lump of burning coal. After the drop, I was well on my way home and back to my comfortable reality.

Reality was sweet and secure. Ryan had cleaned the entire house. I walked into the kitchen and pulled the lid off of a pot of simmering greens. The kids ran down stairs to greet me with hugs and kisses.

"How was your trip?" Ryan kissed me on the lips.

"It was cool. I am just tired from traveling and glad to be home."

"What did your aunt think of Mr. Chow?" I told Ryan before I left that my aunt was meeting me in New York, and we were going to Mr. Chow for drinks and then hang out in New York.

"She loved it." I lied.

"I tried to call you back on Saturday, but your phone went straight to voicemail." Ryan said casually.

"Yeah, I called you before I boarded the train. I tried to call again, but I didn't get reception on the train ride." My answer sounded plausible.

"We missed you mamma."

"I missed you guys too." I dragged my bags into the bedroom and returned to the kitchen to help with dinner. All had returned to normal and normal was not too bad.

On Monday morning, I made breakfast for my family. I scrambled eggs, made bacon, and put biscuits in the oven. Twice during the week, I made dinner using new recipes. Wednesday and Thursday, Ryan and I had level 10 sex. It was almost winter, but I had turned into the spring.

Everyone knows that if you rob a bank, you should keep a low profile. Bank robbers who buy a new Mercedes and fancy clothes the first week after the robbery always get caught. The first rule of robbing a bank is to not get flashy. I am clearly not a successful bank robber, and I was flashing. A week passed and my mid-October fling sent a text message thanking me for his clothes. And that was all.

As I drove through the newly cut corn fields of Jerseyville, I reflected on my short weekend and my entire life. I was all but sure that I would never see Preston again, but I was glad that I met him.

That weekend taught me two valuable lessons. I was not ready to be a farmer or a wife.

My daydream was interrupted by a phone call. It was Kim, my sister-friend from Nashville. Every time I stepped in a pile of shit or fell in a bed of roses she instinctively called me.

"Hello Lady. You were on my mind." Her southern soprano tone made me crave sweet tea.

"What's up girl? It's crazy that you called me. You always catch me when something crazy happens."

"Do tell."

I gave her the PG 13 version of my weekend, and I shared the same version with my Friday happy hour crew. On Saturday, I drafted a mental letter transferring my membership from the First Baptist Couch of Christ. My character had proven to be self unreliant, and I needed a brick and mortar establishment to get my spirit in order. I saw the end of my relationship with Ryan nearing, and I didn't want to end up like the women who sell their soul for soles.

Erin and I sat through church service and I felt happy, proud, sad, guilty, and emotionless all in the same sermon. My spirit had turned into a capitalist. Year after year I wanted God to do 12 percent more for me with less of me. I decided to put more of me into the formula and reverse the trend. I recognized that I was spiritually bankrupt, and I needed more than improvement. And if I thought there were a shortage of good men on Earth just, wait until I get to heaven. I need to get prepared.

It's My Own Fault

THE AIR HAD its panties in a bunch as it wrestled with the drama of this evening's presidential debate, Obama versus Romney and America versus America. It was Tuesday and I needed to talk to Colin about a business matter, but I was hesitant to talk to him on such an important day of politics. I didn't want to hear his views, and I really couldn't fully express mine, but I called him anyway. After the business matter was resolved, sure enough he started talking politics.

"America needs Romney to come through today." Collin truly believed that the world would end if Obama was re-elected.

"All he has to do is tell America how he plans to reverse the failing economy and the Affordable Healthcare Act, and he has a shot." This was my secret way of saying that I didn't believe Romney had a chance.

"Deep down in your heart Jazzmine. You are a republican. I need to vote with you." We laughed, and I laughed harder. I just wanted America to win.

As usual I picked up Cody from day care around 5:30. Ryan called me, and I almost didn't answer. At the last minute, I decided against my better judgement.

"Hey."

"Did you pick Cody up yet?"

"Yes, I just left the daycare."

"Well, I'm at home."

"Oh, OK. You can warm up the beef tips for dinner, and I will make rice when I get home."

"I'm not hungry." His voice went up an octave. "So, you said that you and your aunt met at Mr. Chow's for drinks on Saturday and you took the train back to Philly."

"I sure did say that. Where is this coming from?" Wherever it came from, I wanted it to go back to its home and stay.

"Nowhere. It just didn't make sense to me that you didn't call me until 2 am.

"I tried to call you back. I didn't get reception on the train. When I touched down in New York, my cell phone was dead."

"And you and your aunt and your cousins went to Mr. Chow and took the train back to Philly?"

"Yep and as soon as I charged my phone I called you."

"At 2 in the morning?"

"Yes, when we made it back in Philly at 2 in the morning." I rolled the window down for fresh air. YOLO-gate was making me a little nervous and hot in a bad way.

I didn't join church soon enough for God to deliver me from what would come next. I walked up the steps to my house and heard all of my footsteps. Cassidy was in her room watching television and Ryan was nowhere in sight.

"Hey Cassidy, how was school?"

"It was alright."

"Why was it only alright? Why wasn't it great?" I wanted to stay in Cassidy's room and talk about her day for the next 72 hours, and I was afraid to leave her room.

"Some Bae Bae kids were getting on my nerves. They were talking all day, and they ruined our field trip. None of us can go skating now." Bad behaviors and consequences make the world go round.

The steps leading to the bedrooms began to narrow and the sounds from the television in my bedroom echoed. When I approached the bed, Ryan stepped out of the bed and turned the television volume down from the actual television buttons, and he remained standing.

I could hear his heart beat through his breath, and I suddenly felt the need to have an attorney present for this conversation.

My luggage from the prior week was slightly opened and the purse that I had carried was open.

"So are you positive that you and your cousin and aunt had dinner at Mr. Chow. Think long and hard before you answer." I stared at him and kept my lips fastened, and I searched his eyes for evidence. "And you left New York that night on the train and went back to your room in Philly."

"You are really starting to piss me off. I already told you this." I crossed my arms, rolled my eyes, and shifted my weight to the right side of my body hoping that the right side could support my bold ass lie.

"I know that you don't want to answer these questions Jazzmine because when people are lying they don't want to answer questions."

"So you calling me a liar? You of all people? That's fine with me. I'm done with this conversation. You already have your mind made up. There is no point in me answering your stupid ass questions. We just went for drinks. I don't know why you are making a bid damn deal of this."

"This is why Jazzmine." He produced an email confirmation for Mr. Chow. It showed that I had made dinner reservations for two. The second email asked me to rate my experience. I could get out of that easily.

"Why in the hell are you looking through my emails? I shouldn't have to explain this to you. This is stupid, and I'm about to miss the debate." He smiled a scary smile

"What about this?" He furnished a plastic room key that said, "Thank you for staying in Tribeca. Should you have to explain this?"

He placed the card in my hand, and I looked at it as if it was the first time I had ever seen plastic in card form.

"Yes I should." I took a seat at the edge of the bed and placed my elbow on my thigh. I covered my mouth with my index finger and rested my other digits beneath my chin.

"You are a woman of many words. Did the cat catch your tongue?"

"No, I lied." I did not meet my aunt in New York. I am about to step out for a second. I am going to watch the debate over Erin's house." I headed to the stairs and into Cassidy's room.

"I will be back in an hour pumpkin." Ryan's footsteps were getting closer.

"I am going with you."

"OK. Cassidy keep an eye on your brother for us."

"Let's ride together." I was not feeling Ryan's suggestion at all.

"That's not a good idea. You can follow me." He did not change directions, and he stood at the passenger side of the car. I unlocked the driver's door with the key and left Ryan standing in front of the passenger door. Slowly, I backed out of the driveway.

"I will see you at Erin's." He yelled.

"So who did you go to Mr. Chow with and spend the night with in Tribeca?" He yelled loud enough for me to hear him through the window.

"A man!" I yelled back.

"Now we are getting somewhere!" I heard him scream at the top of his lungs as I pulled into the street and drove away. I called Erin to inform her that she was having company.

"Hey girl, I'm on my way to your house. Ryan is coming with me."

"O...K...I'm home but could you tell me why I am being blessed with you and Ryan's presence at 7:30 at night. I don't mind at all. It's just a little strange."

"It's not strange Erin. It's bad, and I am parking in front of your house now."

Ryan and I marched up Erin's doorstep side by side without making eye contacts, and I knocked on the door. Erin quickly answered.

"Good evening." Her greeting was perfect for a cruise ship greeter and out of place for this moment. Ryan and I walked to the kitchen and took a seat while remaining in strict silence.

"The debate is about to start. Do you guys mind if I turn the TV on? She inquired with a raised eyebrow.

"That's fine. We planned on watching it anyway." I looked at Ryan.

"So your friend had a rendezvous with a man in New York."

Erin coughed, "I think you have jumped to a false conclusion."

"No, I don't think so." He looked at me and then back at Erin.

"Allegedly, Jazzmine went to New York with a man. Let's start there." Erin spoke as if I was not in the room, and she would have held on to his allegation as being a mere suspicion until the end of time.

"No Erin, the jig is up. He knows."

"He knows what?" She was still in character, and I loved her for it.

"He knows that I went to New York with a man."

"Would anyone care for a glass of wine?" We nodded yes, and as she poured the wine the debate began.

There was a verbal character assault, an attack on family values, and a raw throw down on who would make the better leader of the house. All that went on before Romney or Obama could clear their throats. The evening swirled together like a Van Gogh painting then transformed into an Alvin Ailey performance as we used our bodies to create one last scene.

• • •

Two Weeks Later

I told everyone that Ryan and I were done for good. The choir said "Congratulations." Everyone who loved me was so happy for me. They were overly excited to hear the announcement of our break up.

One evening I jogged around my neighborhood and found a full poster of a picture of me and Ryan together and he had written, "I'm sorry for everything," in large letters. There were over 10 of these posters around Benton Park. Ryan had apologized a million times. I called my dad and told him almost everything. I told my father how Ryan apologized to me every night even though I was in the wrong. All he said was, "Hunting ain't no fun when the rabbit got the gun."

This evening was full of peace. The pale apricot walls of my bedroom belonged to me again. The exposed brick wall rested behind my headboard cheerfully. My kids were safe, and they slept in their bedrooms with their pillows propped just right for a good dream. I looked at the ceiling and the North Star dangled from ceiling.

The only person that I had not told that my relationship was over was my second mom Lisa. I didn't think she would believe it was over, but I decided to call her now.

"Hello." She answered on the final ring, and I thought that it was actually the beginning of her voicemail message.

"Lisa it's over."

"What's over?"

"Ryan and I, it's for real this time."

"Yeah right, Ryan just called your daddy earlier. They talked for a long time. You know your daddy didn't talk about the conversation to me, but I'm sure ya'll will work it out."

"No we won't. Not this time. I...I...I got caught cheating."

"You lying."

"No I'm not, and Ryan and I broke up." I gave Lisa a diluted version of my runaway weekend. My delivery was full of energy and excitement.

"After the all that shit that boy has done to you, he will forgive you."

"That's not the point. Lisa, it's not about the man I was with. Hell, I didn't even know him. I did have fun, and I'm not getting back on the porch. I can't do it anymore."

"Is Ryan still living with you?"

"No."

"Where is he?" My bedroom door slowly opened, and I saw Ryan's sad eyes.

"He's...He's in my bedroom. Lisa I will call you back. I ended the call and my deer struck eyes were glued to Ryan. My mouth dropped open and silence fell out.

"You didn't even know him, huh?" He walked slowly towards me.

"Today is the day that I die." That's what the voice in my head said. "And you ain't even finish the new member's class at Friendly Temple." I shook my head.

"I'm kind of relieved that you didn't know him." He walked towards my closet.

"Look at this! Look at this! This is not a skirt that the mother of two children should wear. Look at this dress." He pulled out an assortment of hoochie couture and held the pile of clothes in his hands.

"You've changed Jazzmine. Look at who you have become. You are a mother, but I'm willing to forgive you. We can put this all behind us. I know that you are embarrassed by all of this, but I want you to know that this is nothing compared to the things that I know I have done to you. Remember when I got my vasectomy." I nodded. I did it after Candice got pregnant. She miscarried the baby. I was so afraid of making a mess of my life, and I made the doctor's appointment."

He's not going to kill me tonight. I am going to kill him. I wanted more children, and I begged him not to go through with the procedure. He didn't listen. His ass told me that the reason he wanted a vasectomy was because he didn't believe he could love another child the way he loved Cody. He also said that the thought of having a daughter was worth clipping his nuts. I should have left his black ass then.

Desperation colored the whites of his eyes. Ryan knelt down on the edge of the bed. He was eye level with my knee. "Let's move past

this. I will forgive you. Don't do this to our family, please Jazzmine.
Please." He looked into my confused as hell eyes. He reached in his
pocket and instead of producing a .38 special, he furnished a black
box. "I know you didn't picture this moment like this. Your dad told
me to prepare to hear what I didn't want to hear." My lips unfolded
and dangled into space. I looked like the spooked black coon from
the *Three Stooges.*

"Jazzmine will you marry me?" I shook my head slowly.

"No." Ryan sucked in all of the air in the room and released it. "I
don't want to marry you. I don't trust you, and you don't trust me.
That's a set-up for failure."

"Look, I know that things have not always been good between us,
but they say it gets greater later."

"I have never heard that before. I heard it just gets worse." I
turned my eyes from him.

"Will you at least think about it?"

"Ryan, I don't want to marry you. I want to move on. I want to
date and meet other people." I couldn't believe I said those words.

"I understand. I get it. You have made yourself very clear." He
placed the ring in my hand, and I peeled my eyes from the wall and
placed them on the ring.

"Keep the ring. You deserve it."

This was my wedding proposal, the moment that I had waited for.
We have all seen the Jared Diamond commercials. A passionately in
love man bends on one knee and asks a woman with a beaming smile
for her hand in marriage. She says yes and wipes tears of joy from her
face. The moment is beautiful, heartwarming and full of felicity and
promise. My Jared moment was full of desperation, pain, loss, and
sorrow. It was purely f'd up.

I'd Rather Go Blind

CHRISTMAS SEASON 2012

I worked with Morgan, my manager for the last time of the year. My ride-a-long was more of a celebration than a coaching session. I finished the year ahead of my game and earned a trip to the St. Regis resort in Dana Point, California. We discussed the sales year, the future, and how she had found love in Laguna Beach. Morgan showed me pictures of her Laguna hedge-fund-manager- hottie, and they had been dating strong for almost a year. He enjoyed her time and more importantly he enjoyed spending time with her three children. I hadn't started dating, but Morgan's love story was very encouraging for me. I stayed in my relationship for years with the adage of, "things could be worse." How about things could be better?

The last work day of the year happened to fall on "Perfect Thursday."

St. Louisan's loved three things the Cardinals, toasted ravioli, and Kim Massie. Kim Massie performed every Tuesday and Thursday and when I could make it to a performance. I called it "Perfect Tuesday" or "Perfect Thursday."

Over 100 people crammed into the micro-bar space. There was barely enough room to turn around without knocking over drinks from a nearby table. People lined the entire bar staggered between bar stools. At the front of the bar, at a small pub table sat a group of middle aged mechanics with signs of hard living and missing teeth. Behind the mechanics sat three businessmen in full suits enjoying their scotch and nodding politely to the beat. In the middle of the room, bright eyed college students celebrated a classmate's first legal drink of alcohol. On the dance floor, a girl's night out turned rogue as a group of old friends danced until their faces turned beet red, and their shirts were stained with sweat. And we were all partying on the mountain top at Beale on Broadway with Kim.

I met up with Erin, and we sipped wine and listened to the sound of emotion as the notes flowed through Kim's soul and made a sharp turn to all of the chambers of her heart. The sounds escaped from her lips in a way that made me feel like everyone in the room was my cousin.

I usually made a special request, but today I decided to listen to the songs that reminded everyone else of love. My request would have been too dark and depressing for the occasion. I might have asked her to play that love song by Willie Lynch. She wouldn't know the lyrics by heart of course. And I wouldn't be able to give her a title. I would explain to her that it was that one song about the love of a strong black man that couldn't understand or appreciate the love of a strong black woman. One person after the other passed tips and requested their favorite anthems of love. I decided to celebrate the love in the room. As the night went on, I began to dance until the pain in my heart dropped to the soles of my feet. In the midst of my heavy heart, we still shut the bar down.

Both of my children were away. My daughter spent the holiday with her dad and my son was with his father. It was 3 in the morning, but I was wide awake. I guess my body was tired of dreaming.

My house was empty. I lit a candle on my dresser for company. I stared into the mirror as I wrapped my hair with a light grey and yellow silk scarf, and I smiled. I situated myself in the middle of the bed and gazed at the North Star that dangled from ceiling. My relationship with Ryan ended, and I was ok with it. Ryan wasn't a horrible man. He decided to play the love game with me after the game was over. We were well past regulation and the fans had already left the stadium and the parking lot.

When he asked me to marry him, I could have said yes. Ryan shared himself and my son with another woman not to mention the other incidents of dishonesty that he had been convicted of. I would never hold him as a husband. I would hold him as a hostage. I shared so much with Ryan and wanted to share more while he gave me less than three fifths of who he promised to be. My all was never enough, and he still walked around in misery and pain. It's hard work trying to nurse wounds that are 400 years old, but the Jones's, Miller's, Jackson's, Witherspoon's, Grandberry's, Carlock's, Womack's, Mallard's, and the Blues's seem to carry the torches and the bandages for a lot of us.

I see the light and hope. Men are better than they ever were. Women's choices are also greater than they ever were. We can choose to marry for love and not solely for survival. We marched for that.

Love is all around me and to death do us part. I'm going to love my children, my family, and my friends. My seeds of freedom are safe, and they will not be tended to by a bitter heart.

I am done playing love games. Anybody who wants to play the chess game where the queen has to protect herself from her own king can count me out.

This spring I think I will plant some grass seeds in the bare patches in my yard and flowers.

My thoughts danced until they were tired, and I had one final thought. At the end of the day, I know I have enough heart and hustle to make America-go-round, but I only have enough wind in my heart to blow out my flame......and that is Da'Sho Nuff Blues, but I'm a motherfuckin American and that means that I can sleep, have a dream, and rehearse that shit in the morning.

THE END

Made in the USA
Middletown, DE
19 February 2017